101 Famous Poems

By Roy Cook

Note: this collection contains two extra poems, so there are actually one hundred and three!

ISBN#:   978-1-61104-073-9

Table of Contents

PREFACE

A SPIRIT of daring out of all proportion to any hope
of gain must at times possess a publisher.

You doubtless have heard the story of the *One Hundred and One Best
Songs*; how its publishers printed several hundred thousand books in order
that they might be sold at a price so low as to enable every child to have
one. That, likewise, is the aim of this collection.

To that eminent critic of English verse whose painstaking care in proof-
reading has made this volume authoritative, the publisher acknowledges his
gratitude and debt.

The selections by Emerson, Burroughs, Holmes, Lowell,
Sill, Whittier, Cary, Larcom and Longfellow, are used by permission of and
special arrangement with Houghton- Mifflin Company, authorized
publishers of their works.

Grateful acknowledgment is also made to D. Appleton &
Company, F. W. Bourdillon, The Bobbs-Merrill Company, Charles
Scribner's Sons, Doubleday-Page & Company, Little, Brown & Company,
George H. Doran Company, Lothrop, Lee & Shepard Company, A. P. Watt
& Son, "The Academy,"London, and the Librarian, University of
Edinburgh, without whose kind co-operation this collection could not have
been made,

R. J. COOK, Publisher.
  301. Wabash Ave., Chicago.

1—The Builders

HENRY WADSWORTH LONGFELLOW
(Born February 27, 1807; Died March 24, 1882)

All are architects of Fate,
  Working in these walls of Time;
Some with massive deeds and great,
  Some with ornaments of rhyme.

Nothing useless is, or low;
  Each thing in its place is best;
And what seems but idle show
  Strengthens and supports the rest.

For the structure that we raise,
  Time is with materials filled;
Our todays and yesterdays
  Are the blocks with which we build.

Truly shape and fashion these;
  Leave no yawning gaps between;
Think not, because no man sees.
  Such things will remain unseen.

In the elder days of Art,
  Builders wrought with greatest care
Each minute and unseen part;
  For the gods see everywhere.

Let us do our work as well.
  Both the unseen and the seen;
Make the house where gods may dwell
  Beautiful, entire, and clean.

Else our lives, are incomplete.
  Standing in these walls of Time,
Broken stairways, where the feet
  Stumble, as they seek to climb.

Build today, then, strong and sure,
   With a firm and ample base;
And ascending and secure
   Shall tomorrow find its place.

Thus alone can we attain
   To those turrets, where the eye
Sees the world as one vast plain,
   And one boundless reach of sky.

2—Opportunity

EDWARD R. SILL
(Born, April 29, 1841; Died February 27, 1887)

This I beheld, or dreamed it in a dream:—
There spread a cloud of dust along a plain;
And underneath the cloud, or in it, raged
A furious battle, and men yelled, and swords
Shocked upon swords and shields. A prince's banner
Wavered, then staggered backward, hemmed by foes.

A craven hung along the battle's edge,
And thought, "Had I a sword of keener steel—
That blue blade that the king's son bears—but this
Blunt thing!"—he snapped and flung it from his hand,
And lowering crept away and left the field.

Then came the king's son, wounded, sore bestead.
And weaponless, and saw the broken sword.
Hilt-buried in the dry and trodden sand.
And ran and snatched it, and with battle-shout
Lifted afresh he hewed his enemy down,
And saved a great cause that heroic day.

3—Out to Old Aunt Mary's

JAMES WHITCOMB RILEY
(Born, approx. October 7, 1853; Died July 22, 1916)

Wasn't it pleasant, O brother mine,
In. those old days of the lost sunshine
Of youth—when the Saturday's chores were through.
And the "Sunday's wood"in the kitchen, too,
And we went visiting, "me and you,"
Out to Old Aunt Mary's?

It all comes back so clear today!
Though I am as bald as you are gray—
Out by the barn-lot, and down the lane,
We patter along in the dust again.
As light as the tips of the drops of the rain,
Out to Old Aunt Mary's!

We cross the pasture, and through the wood
Where the old gray snag of the poplar stood.
Where the hammering red-heads hopped awry,
And the buzzard "raised"in the clearing sky.
And lolled and circled, as we went by.
Out to Old Aunt Mary's.
And then in the dust of the road again;
And the teams we met, and the countrymen;
And the long highway, with sunshine spread
As thick as butter on country bread.
Our cares behind, and our hearts ahead
Out to Old Aunt Mary's.

Why, I see her now in the open door.
Where the little gourds grew up the sides, and o'er
The clapboard roof! —And her face—ah, me!
Wasn't it good for a boy to see—
And wasn't it good for a boy to be
Out to Old Aunt Mary's?

The jelly—the jam and the marmalade,
And the cherry and quince "preserves"she made!
And the sweet-sour pickles of peach and pear,
With cinnamon in 'em, and all things rare!—
And the more we ate was the more to spare,
Out to Old Aunt Mary's!

And the old spring-house in the cool green gloom
Of the willow-trees, and the cooler room
Where the swinging-shelves and the crocks were kept-
Where the cream in a golden languor slept
While the waters gurgled and laughed and wept—
Out to Old Aunt Mary's.

And as many a time have you and I—
Barefoot boys in the days gone by-
Knelt, and in tremulous ecstasies
Dipped our lips into sweets like these,—
Memory now is on her knees
Out to Old Aunt Mary's!

And O, my brother, so far away.
This is to tell you she waits today
To welcome us:—Aunt Mary fell
Asleep this morning, whispering, "Tell
The boys to come!"And all is well
Out to Old Aunt Mary's.

4—Each and All

RALPH WALDO EMERSON
(Born May 25, 1803; Died April 27, 1882)

Little thinks, in the field, yon red-cloaked clown
Of thee from the hill-top looking down;
The heifer that lows in the upland farm,
Far-heard, lows not thine ear to charm;
The sexton, tolling his bell at noon,
Deems not that great Napoleon

Stops his horse, and lists with delight,
Whilst his files sweep round yon Alpine height;
Nor knowest thou what argument
Thy life to thy neighbor's creed has lent,
All are needed by each one,—
Nothing is fair or good alone.
I thought the sparrow's note from heaven,
Singing at dawn on the alder bough;
I brought him home, in his nest, at even;
He sings the song, but it cheers not now;
For I did not bring home the river and sky;
He sang to my ear,—they sang to my eye.
The delicate shells lay on the shore;
The bubbles of the latest wave
Fresh pearls to their enamel gave,
And the bellowing of the savage sea
Greeted their safe escape to me.
I wiped away the weeds and foam—
I fetched my sea-born treasures home;
But the poor, unsightly, noisome things
Had left their beauty on the shore
With the sun and the sand and the wild uproar.

The lover watched his graceful maid,
As 'mid the virgin train she strayed,
Nor knew her beauty's best attire
Was woven still by the snow-white choir,
At last she came to his hermitage,
Like the bird from the woodlands to the cage;
The gay enchantment was undone—
A gentle wife, but fairy none.

Then I said, "I covet truth;
Beauty is unripe childhood's cheat;
I leave it behind with the games of youth."
As I spoke, beneath my feet
The ground-pine curled its pretty wreath,
Running over the club-moss burrs;
I inhaled the violet's breath;

Around me stood the oaks and firs;
Pine cones and acorns lay on the ground;
Over me soared the eternal sky,
Full of light and of deity;
Again I saw, again I heard.
The rolling river, the morning bird;
Beauty through my senses stole;
I yielded myself to the perfect whole.

5—The Rhodora

On Being Asked Whence is the Flower

RALPH WALDO EMERSON
(Born May 25, 1803; Died April 27, 1882)

In May, when sea-winds pierced our solitudes,
I found the fresh Rhodora in the woods.
Spreading its leafless blooms in a damp nook,
To please the desert and the sluggish brook.
The purple petals, fallen in the pool,
Made the black water with their beauty gay;
Here might the redbird come his plumes to cool,
And court the flower that cheapens his array.
Rhodora! if the sages ask thee why
This charm is wasted on the earth and sky,
Tell them, dear, that if eyes were made for seeing,
Then Beauty is its own excuse for being:
Why thou wert there, O rival of the rose!
I never thought to ask, I never knew:
But, in my simple ignorance, suppose
The self-same Power that brought me there brought you.

6—Charge of the Light Brigade

ALFRED TENNYSON
(Born August 6, 1809; Died October 6, 1892)

Half a league, half a league,
Half a league onward,
All in the valley of Death
Rode the six hundred.
"Forward, the Light Brigade!
Charge for the guns!"he said:
Into the valley of Death
Rode the six hundred.

"Forward, the Light Brigade!"
Was there a man dismayed?
Not tho' the soldier knew
Some one had blunder'd:
Theirs not to make reply,
Theirs not to reason why,
Theirs but to do and die:
Into the valley of Death
Rode the six hundred.

Cannon to right of them,
Cannon to left of them,
Cannon in front of them
Volleyed and thunder'd;
Storm'd at with shot and shell,
Boldly they rode and well,
Into the jaws of Death,
Into the mouth of Hell,
Rode the six hundred.

Flashed all their sabres bare,
Flashed as they turned in air,
Sab'ring the gunners there,
Charging an army, while
All the world wondered:
Plunged in the battery smoke,

15

Right through the line they broke;
Cossack and Russian
Reeled from the sabre-stroke
Shattered and sundered.
Then they rode back, but not—
Not the six hundred.

Cannon to right of them,
Cannon to left of them,
Cannon behind them
Volleyed and thundered;
Stormed at with shot and shell,
While horse and hero fell,
They that had fought so well.
Came thro' the jaws of Death,
Back from the mouth of Hell,
All that was left of them,
Left of six hundred.
When can their glory fade?
Oh, the wild charge they made!
All the world wondered.
Honor the charge they made!
Honor the Light Brigade,
Noble Six Hundred!

7—The Night Has a Thousand Eyes

FRANCIS WILLIAM BOURDILLON
(Born March 22, 1852; January 13, 1921)

The night has a thousand eyes.
  And the day but one;
Yet the light of the bright world dies
  With the dying sun.
The mind has a thousand eyes.
  And the heart but one;
Yet the light of a whole life dies
  When love is done.

8—The House by the Side of the Road

SAM WALTER FOSS
(Born June 19, 1958; Died February 26, 1911)

There are hermit souls that live withdrawn
  In the place of their self content;
There are souls like stars, that dwell apart,
  In a fellowless firmament;
There are pioneer souls that blaze their paths
  Where highways never ran—
But let me live by the side of the road
  And be a friend to man.

Let me live in a house by the side of the road,
  Where the race of men go by—
The men who are good and the men who are bad,
  As good and as bad as I.
I would not sit in the scorner's seat,
  Or hurl the cynic's ban—
Let me live in a house by the side of the road
  And be a friend to man.

I see from my house by the side of the road,
  By the side of the highway of life,
The men who press with the ardor of hope,
  The men who are faint with the strife.
But I turn not away from their smiles nor their tears,
  Both parts of an infinite plan—
Let me live in a house by the side of the road
  And be a friend to man.

I know there are brook-gladdened meadows ahead
  And mountains of wearisome height;
That the road passes on through the long afternoon
  And stretches away to the night.
But still I rejoice when the travelers rejoice,

17

And weep with the strangers that moan,
Nor live in my house by the side of the road
  Like a man who dwells alone.

Let me live in my house by the side of the road—
  It's here the race of men go by.
They are good, they are bad, they are weak, they are
    strong.
  Wise, foolish—so am I;
Then why should I sit in the scorner's seat,
  Or hurl the cynic's ban?
Let me live in my house by the side of the road
  And be a friend to man.

9—I Have a Rendezvous with Death

ALAN SEEGER
(Born June 22, 1888; Died July 4, 1916)

I have a rendezvous with Death
At some disputed barricade
When spring comes round with rustling shade
And apple blossoms fill the air.
I have a rendezvous with Death
When spring brings back blue days and fair.

It may be he shall take my hand
And lead me into his dark land
And close my eyes and quench my breath;
It may be I shall pass him, still,
I have a rendezvous with Death
On some scarred slope of battered hill,
When spring comes round again this year
And the first meadow flowers appear.

God knows 'twere better to be deep
Pillowed in silk and scented down,
Where love throbs out in blissful sleep,
Pulse nigh to pulse, and breath to breath,

18

Where hushed awakenings are dear . . .
But I've a rendezvous with Death
At midnight in some flaming town,
When spring trips north again this year,
And I to my pledged word am true,
I shall not fail that rendezvous.

10—In Flanders Fields

LIEUT.-COL. JOHN McCRAE
(Born Novermber 30, 1872; Died January 28, 1918)

In Flanders fields the poppies blow
Between the crosses, row on row,
That mark our place; and in the sky
The larks, still bravely singing, fly
Scarce heard amid the guns below.

We are the Dead. Short days ago
We lived, felt dawn, saw sunset glow,
Loved and were loved, and now we lie
In Flanders fields.

Take up our quarrel with the foe;
To you from failing hands we throw
The torch; be yours to hold it high.
If ye break faith with us who die
We shall not sleep, though poppies grow
In Flanders fields.

11—Moonlight

WILLIAM SHAKESPEARE
(Born April 26, 1564; Died April 23; 1616)

How sweet the moonlight sleeps upon this bank!
Here will we sit, and let the sound of music
Creep in our ears: soft stillness, and the night,
Become the touches of sweet harmony.

Sit, Jessica: look, how the floor of heaven
Is thick inlaid with patines of bright gold:
There's not the smallest orb which thou behold'st,
But in his motion like an angel sings,
Still quiring to the young-ey'd cherubins.

12—O Captain! My Captain!

WALT WHITMAN
(Born May 31, 1819; Died March 26, 1892)

O Captain! my Captain! our fearful trip is done;
The ship has weather'd every rack, the prize we sought
   is won;
The port is near, the bells I hear, the people all exulting,
While follow eyes the steady keel, the vessel grim and
   daring:

      But O heart! heart! heart!
       O the bleeding drops of red,
     Where on the deck my Captain lies,
       Fallen cold and dead.

O Captain! my Captain! rise up and hear the bells;
Rise up—for you the flag is flung—for you the bugle
   trills;
For you bouquets and ribbon'd wreaths—for you the
   shores a-crowding;

For you they call, the swaying mass, their eager faces
  turning;

      Here Captain! dear father!
        This arm beneath your head;
      It is some dream that on the deck
        You've fallen cold and dead.

My Captain does not answer, his lips are pale and still;
My father does not feel my arm, he has no pulse nor
  will;
The ship is anchor'd safe and sound, its voyage closed
  and done;
From fearful trip the victor ship comes in with object
  won;

      Exult, O shores, and ring, O bells!
        But I, with mournful tread,
      Walk the deck my Captain lies.
        Fallen cold and dead.

13—The Chambered Nautilus

OLIVER WENDELL HOLMES
(Born August 29, 1809; Died October 7, 1894)

This is the ship of pearl, which, poets feign,
  Sails the unshadowed main,—
  The venturous bark that flings
On the sweet summer wind its purpled wings
In gulfs enchanted, where the Siren sings,
  And coral reefs lie bare,
Where the cold sea-maids rise to sun their streaming
  hair.

Its webs of living gauze no more unfurl;
  Wrecked is the ship of pearl!

And every chambered cell,
Where its dim dreaming life was wont to dwell,
As the frail tenant shaped his growing shell,
　Before thee lies revealed,—
Its irised ceiling rent, its sunless crypt unsealed!

Year after year beheld the silent toil
　That spread his lustrous coil;
　Still, as the spiral grew,
He left the past year's dwelling for the new,
Stole with soft step its shining archway through,
　Built up its idle door.
Stretched in his last-found home, and knew the old no
　　more.

Thanks for the heavenly message brought by thee,
　Child of the wandering sea,
　Cast from her lap, forlorn!
From thy dead lips a clearer note is born
Than ever Triton blew from wreathed horn!
　While on mine ear it rings,
Through the deep caves of thought I hear a voice that
　　sings:—

Build thee more stately mansions, O my soul,
　As the swift seasons roll!
　Leave thy low-vaulted past!
Let each new temple, nobler than the last,
Shut thee from heaven with a dome more vast,
　Till thou at length art free,
Leaving thine outgrown shell by life's unresting sea!

14—Christmas Everywhere

PHILLIPS BROOKS
(Born December 13, 1835; Died January 23, 1893)

Everywhere, everywhere, Christmas tonight!
Christmas in lands of the fir-tree and pine,
Christmas in lands of the palm-tree and vine,
Christmas where snow peaks stand solemn and white,
Christmas where cornfields stand sunny and bright.
Christmas where children are hopeful and gay,
Christmas where old men are patient and gray,
Christmas where peace, like a dove in his flight,
Broods o'er brave men in the thick of the fight;
Everywhere, everywhere, Christmas tonight!

For the Christ-child who comes is the Master of all;
No palace too great, no cottage too small.

15—Little Boy Blue

EUGENE FIELD
(Born September 3, 1850; Died November 4, 1895)

The little toy dog is covered with dust,
  But sturdy and stanch he stands;
And the little toy soldier is red with rust,
  And his musket moulds in his hands.
Time was when the little toy dog was new,
  And the soldier was passing fair,
And that was the time when our Little Boy Blue
  Kissed them and put them there.

"Now, don't you go till I come,"he said,
  "And don't you make any noise!"
So toddling off to his trundle-bed
  He dreamt of the pretty toys.

And as he was dreaming, an angel song
  Awakened our Little Boy Blue,—
Oh, the years are many, the years are long,
  But the little toy friends are true!

Ay, faithful to Little Boy Blue they stand,
  Each in the same old place,
Awaiting the touch of a little hand,
  The smile of a little face.
And they wonder, as waiting these long years through.
  In the dust of that little chair,
What has become of our Little Boy Blue
  Since he kissed them and put them there.

16—The Daffodils

WILLIAM WORDSWORTH
(Born April 7, 1770; Died April 23, 1850)

I wandered lonely as a cloud
  That floats on high o'er vales and hills,
When all at once I saw a crowd,
  A host, of golden daffodils,
Beside the lake, beneath the trees,
Fluttering and dancing in the breeze.

Continuous as the stars that shine
  And twinkle on the Milky Way,
They stretched in never-ending line
  Along the margin of a bay:
Ten thousand saw I at a glance,
Tossing their heads in sprightly dance.

The waves beside them danced, but they
  Outdid the sparkling waves in glee;
A poet could not but be gay
  In such a jocund company.
I gazed, and gazed, but little thought
What wealth the show to me had brought:

24

For oft, when on my couch I lie
  In vacant or in pensive mood,
They flash upon that inward eye
  Which is the bliss of solitude;
And then my heart with pleasure fills.
And dances with the daffodils.

17—June

From "The Vision of Sir Launfal"

JAMES RUSSELL LOWELL
(Born February 22, 1819; Died August 12, 1891)

Over his keys the musing organist,
  Beginning doubtfully and far away,
First lets his fingers wander as they list,
  And builds a bridge from Dreamland for his lay:
Then, as the touch of his loved instrument
  Gives hope and fervor, nearer draws his theme,
First guessed by faint auroral flushes sent
  Along the wavering vista of his dream.
  Not only around our infancy
  Doth heaven with all its splendors lie;
  Daily, with souls that cringe and plot,
  We Sinais climb and know it not.

Over our manhood bend the skies;
  Against our fallen and traitor lives
The great winds utter prophecies;
  With our faint hearts the mountain strives;
Its arms outstretched, the druid wood
  Waits with its benedicite;
And to our age's drowsy blood
  Still shouts the inspiring sea.

Earth gets its price for what Earth gives us;
  The beggar is taxed for a corner to die in,

25

The priest hath his fee who comes and shrives us,
    We bargain for the graves we lie in;
At the devil's booth are all things sold,
Each ounce of dross costs its ounce of gold;
For a cap and bells our lives we pay,
    Bubbles we buy with a whole soul's tasking:
'Tis heaven alone that is given away,
    'Tis only God may be had for the asking;
No price is set on the lavish summer;
June may be had by the poorest comer.

And what is so rare as a day in June?
    Then, if ever, come perfect days;
Then Heaven tries earth if it be in tune,
    And over it softly her warm ear lays;
Whether we look, or whether we listen,
We hear life murmur, or see it glisten;
Every clod feels a stir of might,
    An instinct within it that reaches and towers,
And, groping blindly above it for light,
    Climbs to a soul in grass and flowers;
The flush of life may well be seen
    Thrilling back over hills and valleys;
The cowslip startles in meadows green,
    The buttercup catches the sun in its chalice,
And there's never a leaf nor a blade too mean
    To be some happy creature's palace;
The little bird sits at his door in the sun,
    Atilt like a blossom among the leaves,
And lets his illumined being o'errun
    With the deluge of summer it receives;
His mate feels the eggs beneath her wings,
And the heart in her dumb breast flutters and sings;
He sings to the wide world and she to her nest—
In the nice ear of Nature, which song is the best?

Now is the high-tide of the year,
    And whatever of life hath ebbed away

Comes flooding back with a ripply cheer,
  Into every bare inlet and creek and bay;
Now the heart is so full that a drop overfills it,
We are happy now because God wills it;
No matter how barren the past may have been,
'Tis enough for us now that the leaves are green;
We sit in the warm shade and feel right well
How the sap creeps up and the blossoms swell;
We may shut our eyes, but we cannot help knowing
That skies are clear and grass is growing;
The breeze comes whispering in our ear,
That dandelions are blossoming near,
  That maize has sprouted, that streams are flowing,
That the river is bluer than the sky,
That the robin is plastering his house hard by;
And if the breeze kept the good news back,
For other couriers we should not lack;
  We could guess it all by yon heifer's lowing,—
And hark! how clear bold chanticleer,
Warmed with the new wine of the year,
  Tells all in his lusty crowing!

18—Ode to the West Wind

PERCY BYSSHE SHELLEY
(Born August 4, 1792; Died July 8, 1822)

O wild West Wind, thou breath of Autumn's being,
Thou, from whose unseen presence the leaves dead
Are driven, like ghosts from an enchanter fleeing,
Yellow, and black, and pale, and hectic red,
Pestilence-stricken multitudes! O thou
Who chariotest to their dark wintry bed
The winged seeds, where they lie cold and low,
Each like a corpse within its grave, until
Thine azure sister of the spring shall blow
Her clarion o'er the dreaming earth, and fill
(Driving sweet buds like flocks to feed in air)
With living hues and odors plain and hill:

Wild Spirit, which art moving everywhere;
Destroyer and preserver; hear, oh hear!

Thou on whose stream, 'mid the steep sky's commotion,
Loose clouds like earth's decaying leaves are shed,
Shook from the tangled boughs of heaven and ocean,
Angels of rain and lightning! there are spread
On the blue surface of thine airy surge,
Like the bright hair uplifted from the head
Of some fierce Maenad, ev'n from the dim verge
Of the horizon to the zenith's height,
The locks of the approaching storm. Thou dirge
Of the dying year, to which this closing night
Will be the dome of a vast sepulcher,
Vaulted with all thy congregated might
Of vapours, from whose solid atmosphere
Black ram, and fire, and hail, will burst: oh hear!

Thou who didst waken from his summer-dreams
The blue Mediterranean, where he lay,
Lull'd by the coil of his crystalline streams,
Beside a pumice isle in Baiae's bay,
And saw in sleep old palaces and towers

Quivering within the wave's intenser day,
All overgrown with azure moss, and flowers
So sweet, the sense faints picturing them! Thou
For whose path the Atlantic's level powers
Cleave themselves into chasms, while far below
The sea-blooms and the oozy woods which wear
The sapless foliage of the ocean, know
Thy voice, and suddenly grow gray with fear
And tremble and despoil themselves: oh hear!

If I were a dead leaf thou mightest bear;
If I were a swift cloud to fly with thee;
A wave to pant beneath thy power, and share
The impulse of thy strength, only less free
Than Thou, O uncontrollable! If even

I were as in my boyhood, and could be
The comrade of thy wanderings over heaven,
As then, when to outstrip thy skyey speed
Scarce seem'd a vision,—I would n'er have striven
As thus with thee in prayer in my sore need.
Oh! lift me as a wave, a leaf, a cloud!
I fall upon the thorns of life! I bleed!
A heavy weight of hours has chain'd and bow'd
One too like thee—tameless, and swift, and proud.

Make me thy lyre, ev'n as the forest is:
What if my leaves are falling like its own!
The tumult of thy mighty harmonies
Will take from both a deep autumnal tone,
Sweet though in sadness. Be thou, Spirit fierce,
My spirit! be thou me, impetuous one!
Drive my dead thoughts over the universe,
Like wither'd leaves, to quicken a new birth;
And, by the incantation of this verse,
Scatter, as from an unextinguish'd hearth
Ashes and sparks, my words among mankind!
Be through my lips to unawaken'd earth
The trumpet of a prophecy! O Wind,
If winter comes, can Spring be far behind?

19—The Snowstorm

RALPH WALDO EMERSON
(Born May 25, 1803; Died April 27, 1882)

Announced by all the trumpets of the sky,
Arrives the snow, and, driving o'er the fields,
Seems nowhere to alight: the whited air
Hides hills and woods, the river, and the heaven,
And veils the farmhouse at the garden's end.
The sled and traveler stopped, the courier's feet
Delayed, all friends shut out, the housemates sit
Around the radiant fireplace, enclosed
In a tumultuous privacy of storm.

Come, see the north wind's masonry.
Out of an unseen quarry evermore
Furnished with tile, the fierce artificer
Curves his white bastions with projected roof
Round every windward stake or tree or door.
Speeding, the myriad-handed, his wild work
So fanciful, so savage, naught cares he
For number or proportion. Mockingly
On coop or kennel he hangs Parian wreaths;
A swan-like form invests the hidden thorn;
Fills up the farmer's lane from wall to wall,
Maugre the farmer's sighs; and at the gate
A tapering turret overtops the work.
And when his hours are numbered, and the world
Is all his own, retiring, as he were not,
Leaves, when the sun appears, astonished Art
To mimic in slow structures, stone by stone,
Built in an age, the mad wind's night-work,
The frolic architecture of the snow.

20—To a Skylark

PERCY BYSSHE SHELLEY
(Born August 4, 1792, Died July 8, 1822)

Hail to thee, blithe spirit!
Bird thou never wert,
That from heaven, or near it,
Pourest thy full heart
In profuse strains of unpremeditated art.
Higher still and higher
From the earth thou springest,
Like a cloud of fire;
The blue deep thou wingest,
And singing still dost soar, and soaring ever singest.

In the golden lightning
Of the sunken sun,

O'er which clouds are brightening,
Thou dost float and run,
Like an unbodied joy whose race is just begun.

The pale purple even
Melts around thy flight;
Like a star of heaven,
In the broad daylight
Thou art unseen, but yet I hear thy shrill delight,

Keen as are the arrows
Of that silver sphere,
Whose intense lamp narrows
In the white dawn clear,
Until we hardly see, we feel that it is there.

All the earth and air
With thy voice is loud,
As, when night is bare,
From one lonely cloud
The moon rains out her beams, and heaven is overflowed.

What thou art we know not;
What is most like thee?
From rainbow clouds there flow not
Drops so bright to see,
As from thy presence showers a rain of melody.

Like a poet hidden
In the light of thought,
Singing hymns unbidden,
Till the world is wrought
To sympathy with hopes and fears it heeded not;

Like a high-born maiden
In a palace tower,
Soothing her love-laden
Soul in secret hour
With music sweet as love, which overflows her bower;

Like a glow-worm golden
In a dell of dew,
Scattering unbeholden
Its aerial hue
Among the flowers and grass, which screen it from the
    view;

Like a rose embowered
In its own green leaves,
By warm winds deflowered,
Till the scent it gives
Makes faint with too much sweet these heavy-wingèd
    thieves.

Sound of vernal showers,
On the twinkling grass,
Rain-awakened flowers,
All that ever was
Joyous and clear and fresh thy music doth surpass

Teach us, sprite or bird,
What sweet thoughts are thine!
I have never heard
Praise of love or wine
That panted forth a flood of rapture so divine.

Chorus hymeneal
Or triumphal chant,
Matched with thine, would be all
But an empty vaunt,—
A thing wherein we feel there is some hidden want

What objects are the fountains
Of thy happy strain?
What fields or waves or mountains?
What shapes of sky or plain?
What love of thine own kind? What ignorance of pain?

With thy clear keen joyance
Languor cannot be;
Shadow of annoyance
Never came near thee;
Thou lovest, but ne'er knew love's sad satiety.

Waking or asleep,
Thou of death must deem
Things more true and deep
Than we mortals dream,
Or how could thy notes flow in such a crystal stream?

We look before and after,
And pine for what is not;
Our sincerest laughter
With some pain is fraught;
Our sweetest songs are those that tell of saddest thought.

Yet if we could scorn
Hate and pride and fear;
If we were things born
Not to shed a tear,
I know not how thy joy we ever should come near.

Better than all measures
Of delightful sound,
Better than all treasures
That in books are found,
Thy skill to poet were, thou scorner of the ground!

Teach me half the gladness
That thy brain must know,
Such harmonious madness
From my lips would flow,
The world should listen then, as I am listening now.

21—Hiawatha's Childhood

HENRY WADSWORTH LONGFELLOW
(Born February 27, 1807; Died March 24, 1882)

By the shores of Gitche Gumee,
By the shining Big-Sea-Water,
Stood the wigwam, of Nokomis,
Daughter of the Moon, Nokomis.
Dark behind it rose the forest,
Rose the black and gloomy pine-trees,
Rose the firs with cones upon them;
Bright before it beat the water,
Beat the clear and sunny water,
Beat the shining Big-Sea-Water,
There the wrinkled old Nokomis
Nursed the little Hiawatha,
Rocked him in his linden cradle,
Bedded soft in moss and rushes,
Safely bound with reindeer sinews;
Stilled his fretful wail by saying,
"Hush! the Naked Bear will hear thee
Lulled him into slumber, singing,
"Ewa-yea! my little owlet!
Who is this, that lights the wigwam?
With his great eyes lights the wigwam?
Ewa-yea! my little owlet!"
Many things Nokomis taught him
Of the stars that shine in heaven;
Showed him Ishkoodah, the comet,
Ishkoodah, with fiery tresses;
Showed the Death-Dance of the spirits,
Warriors with their plumes and war-clubs,
Flaring far away to northward
In the frosty nights of winter;
Showed the broad white road in heaven,
Pathway of the ghosts, the shadows,
Running straight across the heavens,
Crowded wiith the ghosts, the shadows.

At the door on summer evenings,
Sat the little Hiawatha;
Heard the whispering of the pine-trees,
Heard the lapping of the waters,
Sounds of music, words of wonder;
"Minne-wawa!"said the pine-trees,
"Mudway-aushka!"said the water.
Saw the fire-fly Wah-wah-taysee,
Flitting through the dusk of evening,
With the twinkle of its candle
Lighting up the brakes and bushes,
And he sang the song of children,
Sang the song Nokomis taught him:
"Wah-wah-taysee, little firefly,
Little, flitting, white-fire insect,
Little, dancing, white-fire creature,
Light me with your little candle,
Ere upon my bed I lay me,
Ere in sleep I close my eyelids!"
Saw the moon rise from the water,
Rippling, rounding from the water,
Saw the flecks and shadows on it,
Whispered, "What is that, Nokomis?"
And the good Nokomis answered:
"Once a warrior, very angry,
Seized his grandmother, and threw her
Up into the sky at midnight;
Right against the moon he threw her;
'Tis her body that you see there."
Saw the rainbow in the heaven,
In the eastern sky the rainbow.
Whispered, "What is that, Nokomis?"
And the good Nokomis answered:
"'Tis the heaven of flowers you see there:
All the wild-flowers of the forest,
All the lilies of the prairie,
When on earth they fade and perish,
Blossom in that heaven above us."
When he heard the owls at midnight,

Hooting, laughing in the forest,
"What is that?"he cried in terror;
"What is that,"he said, "Nokomis?"
And the good Nokomis answered:
"That is but the owl and owlet,
Talking in their native language.
Talking, scolding at each other."
Then the little Hiawatha
Learned of every bird its language,
Learned their names and all their secrets,
How they built their nests in summer,
Where they hid themselves in winter,
Talked with them whene'er he met them,
Called them "Hiawatha's Chickens"
Of all beasts he learned the language,
Learned their names and all their secrets,
How the beavers built their lodges,
Where the squirrels hid their acorns,
How the reindeer ran so swiftly,
Why the rabbit was so timid,
Talked with them whene'er he met them,
Called them "Hiawatha's Brothers."

22—The Happy Warrior

WILLIAM WORDSWORTH
(Born April 7, 1770; Died April 23, 1850)

Who is the happy Warrior? Who is he
That every man in arms should wish to be?
— It is the generous Spirit, who, when brought
Among the tasks of real life, hath wrought
Upon the plan that pleased his boyish thought:
Whose high endeavors are an inward light
That makes the path before him always bright:
Who, with a natural instinct to discern
What knowledge can perform, is diligent to learn;
Abides by this resolve, and stops not there,
But makes his moral being his prime care;

Who, doomed to go in company with Pain,
And Fear, and Bloodshed, miserable train!
Turns his necessity to glorious gain;
In face of these doth exercise a power
Which is our human nature's highest dower;
Controls them and subdues, transmutes, bereaves
Of their bad influence, and their good receives:
By objects, which might force the soul to abate
Her feeling, rendered more compassionate;
Is placable—because occasions rise
So often that demand such sacrifice;
More skillful in self-knowledge, even more pure,
As tempted more; more able, to endure,
As more exposed to suffering and distress;
Thence also, more alive to tenderness.
— 'Tis he whose law is reason; who depends
Upon that law as on the best of friends;
Whence, in a state where men are tempted still
To evil for a guard against worse ill,
And what in quality or act is best
Doth seldom on a right foundation rest,
He labors good on good to fix, and owes
To virtue every triumph that he knows;
— Who, if he rise to station of command,
Rises by open means; and there will stand
On honorable terms, or else retire,
And in himself possess his own desire;
Who comprehends his trust, and to the same
Keeps faithful with a singleness of aim;
And therefore does not stoop, nor lie in wait
For wealth, or honors, or for worldly state;
Whom they must follow; on whose head must fall,
Like showers of manna, if they come at all:
Whose powers shed round him in the common strife,
Or mild concerns of ordinary life,
A constant influence, a peculiar grace;
But who, if he be called upon to face
Some awful moment to which Heaven has joined
Great issues, good or bad for human kind,

Is happy as a Lover; and attired
With sudden brightness, like a Man inspired;
And, through the heat of conflict, keeps the law
In calmness made, and sees what he foresaw;
Or if an unexpected call succeed,
Come when it will, is equal to the need:
— He who, though thus endued as with a sense
And faculty for storm and turbulence,
Is yet a Soul whose master-bias leans
To homefelt pleasures and to gentle scenes;
Sweet images! which, wheresoe'er he be,
Are at his heart; and such fidelity
It is his darling passion to approve;
More brave for this, that he hath much to love:—
'Tis, finally, the Man who lifted high,
Conspicuous object in a Nation's eye,
Or left unthought-of in obscurity,—
Who, with a toward or untoward lot,
Prosperous or adverse, to his wish or not—
Plays, in the many games of life, that one
Where what he most doth value must be won:
Whom neither shape of danger can dismay,
Nor thought of tender happiness betray;
Who, not content that former worth stand fast,
Looks forward, persevering to the last,
From well to better, daily self-surpast:
Who, whether praise of him must walk the earth
Forever, and to noble deeds give birth,
Or he must fall, to sleep without his fame,
And leave a dead unprofitable name—
Finds comfort in himself and in his cause;
And, while the mortal mist is gathering, draws
His breath in confidence of Heaven's applause:
This is the happy Warrior; this is He
That every Man in arms should wish to be.

23—Your Mission

ELLEN H. GATES

If you cannot on the ocean
  Sail among the swiftest fleet,
Rocking on the highest billows,
  Laughing at the storms you meet,
You can stand among the sailors,
  Anchored yet within the bay,
You can lend a hand to help them,
  As they launch their boats away.

If you are too weak to journey
  Up the mountain, steep and high,
You can stand within the valley,
  While the multitudes go by,
You can chant in happy measure,
  As they slowly pass along;
Though they may forget the singer
  They will not forget the song.

If you have not gold and silver
  Ever ready to command,
If you cannot toward the needy
  Reach an ever open hand,
You can visit the afflicted,
  O'er the erring you can weep,
You can be a true disciple,
  Sitting at the Saviour's feet.

If you cannot in the conflict
  Prove yourself a soldier true,
If where the fire and smoke are thickest
  There's no work for you to do.
When the battle-field is silent,
  You can go with careful tread.
You can bear away the wounded,
  You can cover up the dead.

Do not then stand idly waiting
  For some greater work to do;
Fortune is a lazy goddess,
  She will never come to you.
Go and toil in any vineyard,
  Do not fear to do or dare,
If you want a field of labor,
  You can find it anywhere.

24—Not In Vain

EMILY DICKINSON
(Born December 10, 1830; Died May 15, 1886)

If I can stop one heart from breaking,
I shall not live in vain:
If I can ease one life the aching.
Or cool one pain,
Or help one fainting robin
Unto his nest again,
I shall not live in vain.

25—Sheridan's Ride

THOMAS BUCHANAN READ
(Born March 12, 1822; Died May 11, 1872)

Up from the South at break of day,
Bringing to Winchester fresh dismay,
The affrighted air with a shudder bore,
Like a herald in haste, to the chieftain's door,
The terrible grumble, and rumble, and roar,
Telling the battle was on once more,
And Sheridan twenty miles away.

And wider still those billows of war
Thundered along the horizon's bar;
And louder yet into Winchester rolled

The roar of that red sea uncontrolled,
Making the blood of the listener cold,
As he thought of the stake in that fiery fray,
With Sheridan twenty miles away.

But there is a road from Winchester town,
A good, broad highway leading down;
And there, through the flush of the morning light,
A steed as black as the steeds of night,
Was seen to pass, as with eagle flight;
As if h"knew the terrible need,
He stretched away with his utmost speed;
Hills rose and fell; but his heart was gay,
With Sheridan fifteen miles away.

Still sprung from those swift hoofs, thundering South,
The dust, like smoke from the cannon's mouth;
Or the trail of a comet, sweeping faster and faster,
Foreboding to traitors the doom of disaster.
The heart of the steed and the heart of the master
Were beating like prisoners assaulting their walls,
Impatient to be where the battlefield calls;
Every nerve of the charger was strained to full play,
With Sheridan only ten miles away.

Under his spurning feet the road
Like an arrowy Alpine river flowed,
And the landscape sped away behind
Like an ocean flying before the wind,
And the steed, like a barque fed with furnace ire,
Swept on, with his wild eye full of fire.
But lo! he is nearing his heart's desire;
He is snuffing the smoke of the roaring fray,
With Sheridan only five miles away.

The first that the general saw were the groups
Of stragglers, and then the retreating troops;
What was done? What to do? A glance told him both,
Then, striking his spurs, with a terrible oath,

41

He dashed down the line 'mid a storm of huzzas,
And the wave of retreat checked its course there, because
The sight of the master compelled it to pause.
With foam and with dust the black charger was gray;
By the flash of his eye, and the red nostril's play,
He seemed to the whole great army to say,
"I have brought you Sheridan all the way
From Winchester down to save the day!"

Hurrah! Hurrah for Sheridan!
Hurrah! Hurrah for horse and man!
And when their statues are placed on high,
Under the dome of the Union sky,
The American soldier's Temple of Fame;
There with the glorious general's name,
Be it said, in letters both bold and bright,
"Here is the steed that saved the day,
By carrying Sheridan into the fight,
From Winchester, twenty miles away!"

26—The Present Crisis

JAMES RUSSELL LOWELL
(Born February 22, 1819; Died August 12, 1891)

When a deed is done for Freedom, through the broad
    earth's aching breast
Runs a thrill of joy prophetic, trembling on from east to
    west,
And the slave, where'er he cowers, feels the soul within
    him climb
To the awful verge of manhood, as the energy sublime
Of a century bursts full-blossomed on the thorny stem of
    Time.

Through the walls of hut and palace shoots the
    instantaneous throe,
When the travail of the Ages wrings earth's systems to
    and fro;

At the birth of each new Era, with a recognizing start,
Nation wildly looks at nation, standing with mute lips
   apart,
And glad Truth's yet mightier man-child leaps beneath
   the Future's heart.

So the Evil's triumph sendeth, with a terror and a chill,
Under continent to continent, the sense of coming ill,
And the slave, where'er he cowers, feels his sympathies
   with God
In hot tear-drops ebbing earthward, to be drunk up by
   the sod,
Till a corpse crawls round unburied, delving in the
   nobler clod.

For mankind are one in spirit, and an instinct bears
   along,
Round the earth's electric circle, the swift flash of right
   or wrong;
Whether conscious or unconscious, yet Humanity's vast
   frame
Through its ocean-sundered fibres feels the gush of joy
   or shame;—
In the gain or loss of one race all the rest have equal
   claim.

Once to every man and nation comes the moment to
   decide,
In the strife of Truth with Falsehood, for the good or evil
   side;
Some great cause, God's new Messiah, offering each the
   bloom or blight,
Parts the goats upon the left hand and the sheep upon
   the right,
And the choice goes by forever 'twixt that darkness and
   that light.

Hast thou chosen, O my people, on whose party thou
   shalt stand,

Ere the Doom from its worn sandals shakes the dust
   against our land?
Though the cause of Evil prosper, yet 'tis Truth alone is
   strong,
And, albeit she wander outcast now, I see around her
   throng
Troops of beautiful, tall angels, to enshield her from all
   wrong.

Backward look across the ages and the beacon-moments
   see,
That, like peaks of some sunk continent, jut through
   Oblivion's sea;
Not an ear in court or market for the low foreboding cry
Of those Crises, God's stern winnowers, from whose
   feet
   earth's chaff must fly;
Never shows the choice momentous till the judgment
   hath passed by.

Careless seems the great Avenger; history's pages but
   record
One death-grapple in the darkness 'twixt old systems
   and the Word;
Truth forever on the scaffold, Wrong forever on the
   throne,—
Yet that scaffold sways the future, and, behind the dim
   unknown,
Standeth God within the shadow, keeping watch above
   his own.

We see dimly in the Present what is small and what is
   great.
Slow of faith how weak an arm may turn the iron helm
   of fate,
But the soul is still oracular; amid the market's din,
List the ominous stern whisper from the Delphic cave
   within,—

"They enslave their children's children who make
   compromise with sin."

Slavery, the earth-born Cyclops, fellest of the giant
   brood,
Sons of brutish Force and Darkness, who have drenched
   the earth with blood,
Famished in his self-made desert, blinded by our purer
   day,
Gropes in yet unblasted regions for his miserable
   prey;—
Shall we guide his gory fingers where our helpless
   children play?

Then to side with Truth is noble when we share her
   wretched crust,
Ere her cause bring fame and profit, and 'tis prosperous
   to be just;
Then it is the brave man chooses, while the coward
   stands aside,
Doubting in his abject spirit, till his Lord is crucified,
And the multitude make virtue of the faith they had
   denied.

Count me o'er earth's chosen heroes,—they were souls
   that stood alone,
While the men they agonized for hurled the
   contumelious stone,
Stood serene, and down the future saw the golden beam
   incline
To the side of perfect justice, mastered by their faith
   divine,
By one man's plain truth to manhood and to God's
   supreme design.

By the light of burning heretics Christ's bleeding feet I
   track,
Toiling up new Calvaries ever with the cross that turns
   not back,

45

And these mounts of anguish number how each
  generation learned
One new word of that grand *Credo* which in prophet-
  hearts hath burned
Since the first man stood God-conquered with his face to
  heaven upturned.

For humanity sweeps onward: where today the martyr
  stands,
On the morrow crouches Judas with the silver in his
  hands;
Far in front the cross stands ready and the crackling
  fagots burn,
While the hooting mob of yesterday in silent awe return
To glean up the scattered ashes into History's golden
  urn.

'Tis as easy to be heroes as to sit the idle slaves
Of a legendary virtue carved upon our father's graves,
Worshippers of light ancestral make the present light a
  crime;—
Was the Mayflower launched by cowards, steered by
  men behind their time?
Turn those tracks toward Past or Future, that make
  Plymouth Rock sublime?

They were men of present valor, stalwart old iconoclasts,
Unconvinced by axe or gibbet that all virtue was the
  Past's;
But we make their truth our falsehood thinking that hath
  made us free,
Hoarding it in mouldy parchments, while our tender
  spirits flee
The rude grasp of that great impulse which drove them
  across the sea.

They have rights who dare maintain them; we are traitors
  to our sires,

Smothering in their holy ashes Freedom's new-lit
  altar- fires;
Shall we make their creed our jailer? Shall we, in o"
  haste to slay,
From the tombs of the old prophets steal the funeral
  lamps away
To light up the martyr-fagots round the prophets of
  today?

New occasions teach new duties; Time makes ancient
  good uncouth;
They must upward still, and onward, who would keep
  abreast of Truth;
Lo, before us gleam her camp-fires! we ourselves must
  Pilgrims be,
Launch our Mayflower, and steer boldly through the
  desperate winter sea,
Nor attempt the Future's portal with the Past's blood-
  rusted key.

27—Be Strong

MALTBIE DAVENPORT BABCOCK
(Born August 3, 1858; Died May 18, 1901)

Be strong!
We are not here to play, to dream, to drift;
We have hard work to do, and loads to lift;
Shun not the struggle—face it; and 'tis God's gift.

Be strong!
Say not, "The days are evil. Who's to blame?"
And fold the hands and acquiesce—oh shame!
Stand up, speak out, and bravely, in God's name.

Be strong!
It matters not how deep entrenched the wrong,
How hard the battle goes, the day how long;
Faint not—fight on! To-morrow comes the song.

28—Columbus

CINCINNATUS HINER MLLLER
(Born November 10, 1841; Died February 17, 1913)

Behind him lay the gray Azores,
   Behind the Gates of Hercules;
Before him not the ghost of shores,
   Before him only shoreless seas.
The good mate said: "Now must we pray,
   For lo! the very stars are gone.
Brave Adm'r'l, speak; what shall I say?"
   "Why, say: 'Sail on 1 sail on! and on!'"

"My men grow mutinous day by day;
   My men grow ghastly wan and weak."
The stout mate thought of home; a spray
   Of salt wave washed his swarthy cheek.
"What shall I say, brave Adm'r'l, say,
   If we sight naught but seas at dawn?"
"Why, you shall say, at break of day:
   'Sail on! sail on! sail on! and on!'"

They sailed and sailed, as winds might blow,
   Until at last the blanched mate said;
"Why, now not even God would know,
   Should I and all my men fall dead.
These very winds forget their way,
   For God from these dread seas is gone.
Now speak, brave Adm'r'l; speak and say"—
   He said: "Sail on! sail on! and on!"

They sailed. They sailed. Then spake the mate;
   "This mad sea shows his teeth to-night;
He curls his lips, he lies in wait,
   With lifted teeth, as if to bite:
Brave Adm'r'l, say but one good word;
   What shall we do when hope is gone.'"
The words leapt like a leaping sword:
   "Sail on! sail on! sail on! and on!"

Then, pale and worn, he kept his deck,
    And peered through darkness. Ah, that night
Of all dark nights! And then a speck—
    A light! a light! a light! a light!
It grew, a starlit flag unfurled!
    It grew to be Time's burst of dawn.
He gained a world; he gave that world
    Its grandest lesson: "On! sail on!"

29—The Blue and The Gray

FRANCIS MILES FINCH
(Born June 9, 1827; Died July 3!, 1907)

By the flow of the inland river,
    Where the fleets of iron have fled,
Where' the blades of grave grass quiver,
    Asleep are the ranks of the dead;
Under the sod and the dew,
    Waiting the judgment day—
Under the one, the blue;
    Under the other, the gray.

These in the robings of glory,
    Those in the gloom of defeat,
All, with the battle blood gory,
    In the dusk of eternity meet;
Under the sod and the dew,
    Waiting the judgment day—
Under the laurel, the blue;
    Under the willow, the gray.

From the silence of sorrowful hours
The desolate mourners go,
Lovingly laden with flowers
Alike for the friend and the foe;
Under the sod and the dew,
Waiting the judgment day—

49

Under the roses, the blue;
Under the lilies, the gray.

So with an equal splendor
  The morning sun-rays fall,
With a touch impartially tender,
  On the blossoms blooming for all;
Under the sod and the dew,
  Waiting the judgment day—
'Broidered with gold, the blue;
  Mellowed with gold, the gray.

So, when the summer calleth
  On forest and field of grain,
With an equal murmur falleth
  The cooling drip of the rain;
Under the sod and the dew,
  Waiting the judgment day—
Wet with the rain, the blue;
  Wet with the rain, the gray.

Sadly, but not with upbraiding,
  The generous deed was done;
In the storm of the years that are fading,
  No braver battle was won;
Under the sod and the dew,
  Waiting the judgment day—
Under the blossoms, the blue;
  Under the garlands, the gray.

No more shall the war-cry sever,
  Or the winding rivers be red;
They banish our anger forever
  When they laurel the graves of our dead!
Under the sod and the dew,
  Waiting the judgment day—
Love and tears for the blue;
  Tears and love for the gray.

30—Recessional

RUDYARD KIPLING
(Born December 30, 1865; Death January 18, 1936)

God of our fathers, known of old—
  Lord of our far-flung battle line—
Beneath whose awful hand we hold
  Dominion over palm and pine—
Lord God of Hosts, be with us yet,
  Lest we forget—lest we forget!

The tumult and the shouting dies—
  The Captains and the Kings depart—
Still stands Thine ancient sacrifice,
  An humble and a contrite heart.
Lord God of Hosts, be with us yet,
  Lest we forget—lest we forget!

Far-called, our navies melt away—
  On dune and headland sinks the fire—
Lo, all our pomp of yesterday
  Is one with Nineveh and Tyre!
Judge of the Nations, spare us yet,
  Lest we forget —lest we forget!

If, drunk with sight of power, we loose
  Wild tongues that have not Thee in awe—
Such boasting as the Gentiles use,
  Or lesser breeds without the Law—
Lord God of Hosts, be with us yet,
  Lest we forget—lest we forget!

For heathen heart that puts her trust
  In reeking tube and iron shard—
All valiant dust that builds on dust,
  And guarding, calls not Thee to guard,
For frantic boast and foolish word,
  Thy Mercy on Thy People, Lord! Amen!

31—The Cloud

PERCY BYSSHE SHELLEY
(Born August 4, 1792; Died July 8, 1822)

I bring fresh showers for the thirsting flowers,
   From the seas and the streams;
I bear light shade for the leaves when laid
   In their noonday dreams.
From my wings are shaken the dews that waken
   The sweet buds every one,
When rocked to rest on their mother's breast,
   As she dances about the sun.
I wield the flail of the lashing hail,
   And whiten the green plains under;
And then again I dissolve it in rain,
   And laugh as I pass in thunder.

I sift the snow on the mountains below,
   And their great pines groan aghast;
And all the night 'tis my pillow white,
   While I sleep in the arms of the blast.
Sublime on the towers of my skyey bowers,
   Lightning, my pilot, sits;
In a cavern under is fettered the thunder,
   It struggles and howls at fits;
Over earth and ocean, with gentle motion,
   This pilot is guiding me,
Lured by the love of the genii that move
   In the depths of the purple sea;
Over the rills and the crags and the hills,
   Over the lakes and the plains,
Wherever he dream, under mountain or stream,
   The Spirit he loves remains;
And I all the while bask in heaven's blue smile,
   Whilst he is dissolving in rains.

The sanguine sunrise, with his meteor eyes,
   And his burning plumes outspread,
Leaps on the back of my sailing rack,

When the morning star shines dead:
As on the jag of a mountain crag
  Which an earthquake rocks and swings,
An eagle alit one moment may sit
  In the light of its golden wings.
And when sunset may breathe, from the lit sea beneath,
  Its ardors of rest and of love,
And the crimson pall of eve may fall
  From the depth of heaven above,
With wings folded I rest on mine airy nest,
  As still as a brooding dove.

That orbèd maiden with white fire laden,
  Whom mortals call the moon,
Glides glimmering o'er my fleecelike floor,
  By the midnight breezes strewn;
And wherever the beat of her unseen feet,
  Which only the angels hear,
May have broken the woof of my tent's thin roof,
  The stars peep behind her and peer.
And I laugh to see them whirl and flee
  Like a swarm of golden bees,
When I widen the rent in my wind-built tent,—
  Till the calm rivers, lakes, and seas,
Like strips of the sky fallen through me on high,
  Are each paved with the moon and these.

I bind the sun's throne with a burning zone,
  And the moon's with a girdle of pearl;
The volcanoes are dim, and the stars reel and swim,
  When the whirlwinds my banner unfurl.
From cape to cape, with a bridge-like shape,
  Over a torrent sea,
Sunbeam-proof, I hang like a roof,—
  The mountains its columns be.
The triumphal arch through which I march
  With hurricane, fire, and snow,
When the powers of the air are chained to my chair,
  Is the million-colored bow;

The sphere-fire above its soft colors wove,
  While the moist earth was laughing below.

I am the daughter of earth and water,
  And the nursling of the sky;
I pass through the pores of the ocean and shores;
  I change, but I cannot die.
For after the rain, when, with never a stain,
  The pavilion of heaven is bare,
And the winds and sunbeams, with their convex gleams,
  Build up the blue dome of air,
I silently laugh at my own cenotaph,
  And out of the caverns of rain,
Like a child from the womb, like a ghost from the tomb,
  I arise and unbuild it again.

32—How Did You Die?

EDMUND VANCE COOKE
(Born June 5, 1866; Died December 18, 1932)

Did you tackle that trouble that came your way
  With a resolute heart and cheerful?
Or hide your face from the light of day
  With a craven soul and fearful?
Oh, a trouble's a ton, or a trouble's an ounce,
  Or a trouble is what you make it.
And it isn't the fact that you're hurt that counts,
  But only how did you take it?

You are beaten to earth? Well, well, what's that?
  Come up with a smiling face.
It's nothing against you to fall down flat,
  But to lie there—that's disgrace.
The harder you're thrown, why the higher you bounce;
  Be proud of your blackened eye!
It isn't the fact that you're licked that counts;
  It's how did you fight and why?

54

And though you be done to death, what then?
  If you battled the best you could;
If you played your part in the world of men,
  Why, the Critic will call it good.
Death comes with a crawl, or comes with a pounce,
  And whether he's slow or spry,
It isn't the fact that you're dead that counts,
  But only, how did you die?

33—Wolsey's Farewell to His Greatness

JOHN FLETCHER
(Born December 20, 1579; Died August 28(?), 1625)

Farewell! a long farewell to all my greatness!
This is the state of man: today he puts forth
The tender leaves of hope, to-morrow blossoms,
And bears his blushing honors thick upon him;
The third day comes a frost, a killing frost;
And—when he thinks, good easy man, full surely
His greatness is a-ripening—nips his root,
And then he falls, as I do. I have ventured,
Like little wanton boys that swim on bladders,
This many summers in a sea of glory,
But far beyond my depth; my high blown pride
At length broke under me, and now has left me,
Weary and old with service, to the mercy
Of a rude stream, that must forever hide me.
Vain pomp and glory of this world, I hate ye!
I feel my heart new-opened. Oh! How wretched
Is that poor man that hangs on princes' favors!
There is, betwixt that smile we would aspire to,
That sweet aspect of princes, and their ruin,
More pangs and fears than wars or women have;
And when he falls, he falls like Lucifer,
Never to hope again.

34—The Blessed Damozel

DANTE GABRIEL ROSSETTI
(Born May 12, 1828; Died April 9, 1882)

The blessed damozel leaned out
  From the gold bar of heaven;
Her eyes were deeper than the depth
  Of waters stilled at even;
She had three lilies in her hand,
  And the stars in her hair were seven.

Her robe, ungirt from clasp to hem,
  No wrought flowers did adorn,
But a white rose of Mary's gift,
  For service meetly worn;
Her hair that lay along her back
  Was yellow like ripe corn.

Her seemed she scarce had been a day
  One of God's choristers;
The wonder was not yet quite gone
  From that still look of hers;
Albeit, to them she left, her day
  Had counted as ten years.

(To one, It is ten years of years,
  . . . Yet now, and in this place,
Surely she lean'd o'er me— her hair
  Fell all about my face, . . .
Nothing: the autumn fall of leaves.
  The whole year sets apace.)

It was the rampart of God's house
  That she was standing on;
By God built over the sheer depth
  The which is Space begun;
So high, that looking downward thence
  She scarce could see the sun.

It lies in heaven, across the flood
  Of ether, as a bridge.
Beneath, the tides of day and night
  With flame and darkness ridge
The void, as low as where this earth
  Spins like a fretful midge.

Around her, lovers, newly met
  'Mid deathless love's acclaims
Spake evermore among themselves
  Their heart-remember'd names;
And the souls mounting up to God
  Went by her like thin flames.

And still she bowed herself and stooped
  Out of the circling charm;
Until her bosom must have made
  The bar she leaned on warm,
And the lilies lay as if asleep
  Along her bended arm.

From the fixed place of heaven she saw
  Time like a pulse shake fierce
Through all the worlds. Her gaze still strove
  Within the gulf to pierce
The path; and now she spoke as when
  The stars sang in their spheres.

The sun was gone now; the curled moon
  Was like a little feather
Fluttering far down the gulf; and now
  She spoke through the still weather.
Her voice was like the voice the stars
  Had when they sang together.

(Ah, sweet! even now, in that bird's song,
  Strove not her accents there,
Fain to be hearkened f When those bells
  Possessed the mid-day air,

Strove not her steps to reach my side
  Down all the echoing stair?)

"I wish that he were come to me,
  For he will come,"she said.
Have I not prayed in heaven?—on earth,
  Lord, Lord, has he not prayed?
Are not two prayers a perfect strength?
  And shall I feel afraid?

"When round his head the aureole clings,
  And he is clothed in white,
I'll take his hand and go with him
  To the deep wells of light;
As unto a stream we will step down,
  And bathe there in God's sight.

"We two will stand beside that shrine,
  Occult, withheld, untrod,
Whose lamps are stirred continually
  With prayer sent up to God;
And see our old prayers, granted, melt
  Each like a little cloud.

"We two will lie I' the shadow of
  That living mystic tree,
Within whose secret growth the Dove
  Is sometimes felt to be,
While every leaf that His plumes touch
  Saith His Name audibly.

"And I myself will teach to him,
  I myself, lying so,
The songs I sing here; which his voice
  Shall pause in, hushed and slow,
And find some knowledge at each pause,
  Or some new thing to know."

(Alas! We two, we two, thou say'st!
 Yea, one was thou with me
That once of old. But shall God lift
 To endless unity
The soul whose likeness with thy soul
 Was but its love for thee?)

"We two,"she said, "will seek the groves
 Where the Lady Mary is,
With her five handmaidens, whose names
 Are five sweet symphonies,
Cecily, Gertrude, Magdalen,
 Margaret, and Rosalys.

"Circlewise sit they, with bound locks
 And foreheads garlanded;
Into the fine cloth, white like flame,
 Weaving the golden thread,
To fashion the birth-robes for them
 Who are just bom, being dead.

"He shall fear, haply, and be dumb;
 Then will I lay my cheek
To his, and tell about our love,
 Not once abashed or weak:
And the dear Mother will approve
 My pride, and let me speak.

"Herself shall bring us, hand in hand,
 To Him round whom all souls
Kneel, the clear-ranged unnumbered heads
 Bowed with their aureoles:
And angels meeting us shall sing
 To their citherns and citoles.

"There will I ask of Christ the Lord
 Thus much for him and me: —
Only to live as once on earth
 With Love—only to be,

59

As then awhile, forever now
  Together, I and he."

She gazed and listened, and then said,
  Less sad of speech than mild—
"All this is when he comes."She ceased.
  The light thrilled towards her, filled
With angels in strong level flight.
  Her eyes prayed, and she smiled.

(I saw her smile.) But soon their path
  Was vague in distant spheres:
And then she cast her arms along
  The golden barriers,
And laid her face between her hands
  And wept. (I heard her tears.)

35—America for Me

HENRY VAN DYKE
(Born November 10, 1852; April 10, 1933)

'Tis fine to see the Old World, and travel up and down
Among the famous palaces and cities of renown,
To admire the crumbly castles and the statues of the
  kings,—
But now I think I've had enough of antiquated things.

So it's home again, and home again, America for me!
My heart is turning home again, and there I long to be,
In the land of youth and freedom beyond the ocean bars
Where the air is full of sunlight and the flag is full of
  stars.

Oh, London is a man's town, there's power in the air;
And Paris is a woman's town, with flowers in her hair;
And it's sweet to dream in Venice, and it's great to study
  Rome;
But when it comes to living there is no place like home.

I like the German fir-woods, in green battalions drilled;
I like the gardens of Versailles with flashing fountains
    filled;
But, oh, to take your hand, my dear, and ramble for a
    day
In the friendly western woodland where Nature has her
    way!

I know that Europe's wonderful, yet something seems to
    lack:
The Past is too much with her, and the people looking
    back.
But the glory of the Present is to make the Future free,—
We love our land for what she is and what she is to be.

Oh, it's home again, and home again, America for me!
I want a ship that's westward bound to plough the
    rolling sea.
To the blessed Land of Room Enough beyond the ocean
    bars,
Where the air is full of sunlight and the flag is full of
    stars.

36—Song of the Shirt

THOMAS HOOD
(Born May 23, 1799; Died May 3, 1845)

With fingers weary and worn,
    With eyelids heavy and red,
A woman sat in unwomanly rags,
    Plying her needle and thread—
Stitch! stitch! stitch!
    In poverty, hunger and dirt,
And still with a voice of dolorous pitch
    She sang the "Song of the Shirt!"
"Work! work! work!
    While the cock is crowing aloof!
And work—work—work,

Till the stars shine through the roof!
It's oh! To be a slave
  Along with the barbarous Turk,
Where a woman has never a soul to save,
  If this is Christian work!

"Work—work—work
  Till the brain begins to swim;
Work—work—work
  Till the eyes are heavy and dim!
Seam, and gusset, and band,
  Band, and gusset, and seam,
Till over the buttons I fall asleep,
  And sew them on in a dream!
"O men, with sisters dear!
  O men, with mothers and wives!
It is not linen you're wearing out,
  But human creatures' lives!
Stitch—stitch'—stitch!
  In poverty, hunger, and dirt,—
Sewing at once, with a double thread,
  A shroud as well as a shirt!

"But why do I talk of Death,—
  That phantom of grisly bone?
I hardly fear his terrible shape,
  It seems so like my own,—
  It seems so like my own,
Because of the fasts I keep;
  O God! that bread should be so dear,
And flesh and blood so cheap!
"Work! work! work!
  My labor never flags;
And what are its wages? A bed of straw,
  A crust of bread—and rags,
That shattered roof—and this naked floor—
  A table—a broken chair—
And a wall so blank, my shadow I thank
  For sometimes falling there!

"Work—work—work!
  From weary chime to chime!
Work— work—work!
  As prisoners work for crime!
Band, and gusset, and seam,
  Seam, and gusset, and band,—
Till the heart is sick and the brain benumbed,
  As well as the weary hand.

"Work—work—work!
  In the dull December light!
And work—work—work!
  When the weather is warm and bright!
While underneath the eaves
  The brooding swallows cling,
As if to show me their sunny backs.
  And twit me with the spring.
"Oh, but to breathe the breath
  Of the cowslip and primrose sweet,—
With the sky above my head,
  And the grass beneath my feet!
For only one short hour
  To feel as I used to feel,
Before I knew the woes of want
  And the walk that costs a meal!
"Oh, but for one short hour,—
  A respite, however brief!
No blessed leisure for love or hope,
  But only time for grief!
A little weeping would ease my heart;
  But in their briny bed
My tears must stop, for every drop
Hinders needle and thread!"

With fingers weary and worn,
  With eyelids heavy and red,
A woman sat in unwomanly rags,
  Plying her needle and thread,—

Stitch! stitch! stitch!
   In poverty, hunger and dirt;
And still with a voice of dolorous pitch—
Would that its tone could reach the rich! —
   She sang the "Song of the Shirt."

37—Mercy

WILLIAM SHAKESPEARE
(Born April 26, 1564; Died April 23; 1616)

The quality of mercy is not strained;
It droppeth as the gentle rain from heaven
Upon the place beneath: it is twice blest,—
It blesseth him that gives and him that takes:
'Tis mightiest in the mightiest; it becomes
The thronèd monarch better than his crown:
His sceptre shows the force of temporal power,
The attribute to awe and majesty,
Wherein doth sit the dread and fear of kings;
But mercy is above this sceptred sway,—
It is enthroned in the hearts of kings,
It is an attribute to God himself;
And earthly power doth then show likest God's,
When mercy seasons justice.

38—The Opening of the Piano

OLIVER WENDELL HOLMES
(Born August 29, 1809; Died October 7, 1894)

In the little southern parlor of the house you may have
   seen
With the gambrel-roof, and the gable looking westward
   to the green,
At the side toward the sunset, with the window on its
   right,
Stood the London-made piano I am dreaming of tonight!

Ah me! how I remember the evening when it came!
What a cry of eager voices, what a group of cheeks in
  flame,
When the wondrous box was opened that had come from
  overseas,
With its smell of mastic-varnish and its flash of ivory
  keys!

Then the children all grew fretful in the restlessness of
  joy;
For the boy would push his sister, and the sister crowd
  the boy,
Till the father asked for quiet in his grave paternal way,
But the mother hushed the tumult with the words, "Now,
  Mary, play."

For the dear soul knew that music was a very sovereign
  balm;
She had sprinkled it over Sorrow and seen its brow grow
  calm,
In the days of tender harpsichords with tapping tinkling
  quills,
Or carolling to her spinet with its thin metallic thrills.

So Mary, the household minstrel, who always loved to
  please,
Sat down to the new "Clementi,"and struck the
  glittering keys.
Hushed were the children's voices, and every eye grew
  dim,
As, floating from lip and finger, arose the "Vesper
  Hymn."

Catharine, child of a neighbor, curly and rosy-red,
(Wedded since, and a widow,—something like ten
  years dead),
Hearing a gush of music such as none before,

Steals from her mother's chamber and peeps at the open
  door

Just as the "Jubilate"in threaded whisper dies,
"Open itl open it, lady!"the little maiden cries,
(For she thought it was a singing creature caged in a box
  she heard),
"Open it! open it, lady! and let me see the birdi."

39—Sonnet
"The World is Too Much With Us"

WILLIAM WORDSWORTH
(Born April 7, 1770; Died April 23, 1850)

The World is too much with us; late and soon,
Getting and spending, we lay waste our powers;
Little we see in Nature that is ours;
We have given our hearts away, a sordid boon!
This sea that bares her bosom to the moon;
The winds that will be howling at all hours,
And are up-gathered now like sleeping flowers;
For this, for everything, we are out of tune;
It moves us not.— Great God! I'd rather be
A Pagan suckled in a creed outworn,
So might I, standing on this pleasant lea,
Have glimpses that would make me less forlorn;
Have sight of Proteus rising from the sea,
Or hear old Triton blow his wreathed horn.

40—The Duel

EUGENE FIELD

(Born September 3, 1850; Died November 4, 1895)

The gingham dog and the calico cat
Side by side on the table sat;
'T was half-past twelve, and (what do you think!)
Nor one nor t' other had slept a wink!
  The old Dutch clock and the Chinese plate
  Appeared to know as sure as fate
There was going to be a terrible spat.
  (I wasn't there; I simply state
  What was told to me by the Chinese plate!)

The gingham dog went "bow-wow-wow!"
And the calico cat replied "mee-ow!"
The air was littered, an hour or so,
With bits of gingham and calico,
  While the old Dutch clock in the chimney-place
  Up with its hands before its face,
For it always dreaded a family row!
  (Never mind: I'm only telling you
  What the old Dutch clock declares is true!)

The Chinese plate looked very blue,
And wailed, "Oh, dear! What shall we do!"
But the gingham dog and the calico cat
Wallowed this way and tumbled that,
  Employing every tooth and claw
  In the awfullest way you ever saw—
And, oh! How the gingham and calico flew!
  Don't fancy I exaggerate—
  I got my news from the Chinese plate!)

Next morning where the two had sat
They found no trace of dog or cat;
And some folks think unto this day
That burglars stole that pair away!
  But the truth about the cat and pup

Is this: they ate each other up!
Now what do you really think of that!
(The old Dutch clock it told me so,
And that is how I came to know.)

41—Song of the Chattahoochee

SIDNEY LANIER
(Born February 3, 1842; Died September 7, 1881)

Out of the hills of Habersham,
Down the valleys of Hall,
I hurry amain to reach the plain,
Run the rapid and leap the fall,
Split at the rock and together again,
Accept my bed, or narrow or wide,
And flee from folly on every side
With a lover's pain to attain the plain
Far from the hills of Habersham,
Far from the valleys of Hall,

All down the hills of Habersham,
All through the valleys of Hall,
The rushes cried *Abide, abide,*
The willful waterweeds held me thrall,
The laving laurel turned my tide,
The ferns and the fondling grass said Stay,
The dewberry dipped for to work delay,
And the little reeds sighed *Abide, abide,*
Here in the-kills of Habersham,
Here in the valleys of Hall

High o'er the hills of Habersham,
Veiling the valleys of Hall,
The hickory told me manifold
Fair tales of shade, the poplar tall
Wrought me her shadowy self to hold,
The chestnut, the oak, the walnut, the pine,
Overleaning, with flickering meaning and sign,

Said, *Pass not, so cold, these manifold*
Deep shades of the hills of Habersham,
These glades in the valleys of Hall,

And oft in the hills of Habersham,
And oft in the valleys of Hall,
The white quartz shone, and the smooth brook-stone
Did bar me of passage with friendly brawl,
And many a luminous jewel lone—
Crystals clear or a-cloud with mist,
Ruby, garnet and amethyst—
Made lures with the lights of streaming stone
In the clefts of the hills of Habersham,
In the beds of the valleys of Hall.

But oh, not the hills of Habersham,
And oh, not the valleys of Hall
Avail: I am fain to water the plain.
Downward the voices of Duty call—
Downward, to toil and be mixed with the main;
The dry fields burn, and the mills are to turn,
And a myriad flowers mortally yearn,
And the lordly main beyond the plain
Calls o'er the hills of Habersham,
Calls through the valleys of Hall.

42—Ode on Intimations of Immortality

From Recollections of Early Childhood

WILLIAM WORDSWORTH
(Born April 7, 1770; Died April 23, 1850)

There was a time when meadow, grove, and stream,
The earth, and every common sight,
To me did seem
Apparelled in celestial light,
The glory and the freshness of a dream.
It is not now as it hath been of yore;—

Turn wheresoe'er I may,
By night or day,
The things which I have seen I now can see no more.

The rainbow comes and goes,
And lovely is the rose;
The moon doth with delight
Look round her when the heavens are bare;
Waters on a starry night
Are beautiful and fair;
The sunshine is a glorious birth;
But yet I know, where'er I go,
That there hath past away a glory from the earth.

Now, while the birds thus sing a joyous song,
And while the young lambs bound
As to the tabor's sound,
To me alone there came a thought of grief:
A timely utterance gave that thought relief,
And I again am strong.
The cataracts blow their trumpets from the steep;—
No more shall grief of mine the season wrong:
I hear the echoes through the mountains throng.
The winds come to me from the fields of sleep,
And all the earth is gay;
Land and sea

Give themselves up to jollity,
And with the heart of May
Doth every beast keep holiday;—
Thou child of joy
Shout round me, let me hear thy shouts, thou happy
  shepherd-boy!

Ye blessed Creatures, I have heard the call
  Ye to each other make; I see
The heavens laugh with you in your jubilee;
  My heart is at your festival,
  My head hath its coronal,

The fullness of your bliss, I feel—I feel it all.
　Oh evil day! If I were sullen
　While Earth herself is adorning
　　This sweet May-morning;
　And the children are culling
　　On every side
　In a thousand valleys far and wide,
　Fresh flowers; while the sun shines warm
And the babe leaps up on his mother's arm:—
　I hear, I hear, with joy I hear!
　—But there's a tree, of many, one,
A single field which I have look'd upon,
Both of them speak of something that is gone:
　　The pansy at my feet
　　Doth the same tale repeat:
Whither is fled the visionary gleam?
Where is it now, the glory and the dream?
Our birth is but a sleep and a forgetting;
The Soul that rises with us, our life's Star,
　Hath had elsewhere its setting
　　And Cometh from afar;
　Not in entire forgetfulness,
　And not in utter nakedness,
But trailing clouds of glory do we come
　　From God, who is our home:
Heaven lies about us in our infancy!
Shades of the prison-house begin to close
　Upon the growing Boy,
But he beholds the light, and whence it flows,
　He sees it in his joy;
The Youth, who daily farther from the east
　Must travel, still is Nature's priest,
　　And by the vision splendid
　　Is on his way attended;
At length the Man perceives it die away,
And fade into the light of common day.
Earth fills her lap with pleasures of her own;
Yearnings she hath in her own natural kind,
And, even with something of a mother's mind,

And no unworthy aim,
　The homely nurse doth all she can
To make her foster-child, her inmate, Man,
　Forget the glories he hath known,
And that imperial palace whence he came.

Behold the Child among his new-born blisses,
A six years' darling of a pigmy size!
See, where 'mid work of his own hand he lies,
Fretted by sallies of his mother's kisses,
With light upon him from his father's eyes!
See, at his feet, some little plan or chart,
Some fragment from his dream of human life,
Shaped by himself with newly-learned art;
　A wedding or a festival,
　A mourning or a funeral;
　　And this hath now his heart,
　And unto this he frames his song;
　　Then will he fit his tongue
To dialogues of business, love, or strife;
　But it will not be long
　Ere this be thrown aside,
　And with new joy and pride
The little actor cons another part;
Filling from time to time his 'humorous stage'
With all the persons, down to palsied Age,
That Life brings with her in her equipage;
　As if his whole vocation
　Were endless imitation.

Thou, whose exterior semblance doth belie
　Thy soul's immensity;
Thou best philosopher, who yet dost keep
Thy heritage, thou eye among the blind,
That, deaf and silent, read'st the eternal deep,
Haunted forever by the eternal Mind,—
　Mighty Prophet! Seer blest!
　On whom those truths do rest
Which we are toiling all our lives to find,

In darkness lost, the darkness of the grave;
Thou, over whom thy Immortality
Broods like the day, a master o'er a slave,
A Presence which is not to be put by;
Thou little child, yet glorious in the might
Of heaven-born freedom on thy being's height,
Why with such earnest pains dost thou provoke
The years to bring the inevitable yoke,
Thus blindly with thy blessedness at strife?
Full soon thy soul shall have her earthly freight,
And custom lie upon thee with a weight
Heavy as frost, and deep almost as life!

    O joy! That in our embers
    Is something that doth live,
    That nature yet remembers
    What was so fugitive!
The thought of our past years in me doth breed
Perpetual benediction: not indeed
For that which is most worthy to be blest,
Delight and liberty, the simple creed
Of Childhood, whether busy or at rest,
With new-fledged hope still fluttering in her breast:
    Not for these I raise
    The song of thanks and praise;
  But for those obstinate questionings
  Of sense and outward things,
  Fallings from us, vanishings;
  Blank misgivings of a creature
Moving about in worlds not realized,
High instincts, before which our mortal nature
Did tremble like a guilty thing surprised:
  But for those first affections,
  Those shadowy recollections,
    Which, be they what they may,
Are yet the fountain-light of all our day,
Are yet a master-light of all our seeing;
    Uphold us, cherish, and have power to make
Our noisy years seem moments in the being

Of the eternal Silence: truths that wake,
    To perish never;
Which neither listlessness, nor mad endeavour,
    Nor man nor boy
Nor all that is at enmity with joy,
Can utterly abolish or destroy!
    Hence in a season of calm weather,
      Though inland far we be,
Our souls have sight of that immortal sea
      Which brought us hither;
    Can in a moment travel thither,
And see the children sport upon the shore,
And hear the mighty waters rolling evermore.

Then sing, ye birds, sing, sing a joyous song!
    And let the young lambs bound
    As to the tabor's sound!
  We in thought will join your throng
    Ye that pipe and ye that play,
    Ye that through your hearts today
    Feel the gladness of the May!
What though the radiance which was once so bright
Be now for ever taken from my sight,
  Though nothing can bring back the hour
Of splendour in the grass, of glory in the flower;
    We will grieve not, rather find
    Strength in what remains behind;
    In the primal sympathy
    Which having been must ever be;
    In the soothing thoughts that spring
    Out of human suffering;
    In the faith that looks through death,
In years that bring the philosophic mind.

And O, ye Fountains, Meadows, Hills, and Groves,
Forbode not any severing of our loves!
Yet in my heart of hearts I feel your might;
I only have relinquished one delight
To live beneath your more habitual sway:

I love the brooks which down their channels fret
Even more than when I tripped lightly as they;
The innocent brightness of a new-born day
      Is lovely yet;
The clouds that gather round the setting sun
Do take a sober colouring from an eye
That hath kept watch o'er man's mortality;
Another race hath been, and other palms are won.
Thanks to the human heart by which we live,
Thanks to its tenderness, its joys, and fears,
To me the meanest flower that blows can give
Thoughts that do often lie too deep for tears.

43—Each In His Own Tongue

WILLIAM HERBERT CARRUTH
(Born April 5, 1859; Died 1924)

A fire-mist and a planet,
  A crystal and a cell,
A jelly-fish and a saurian,
  And caves where the cave-men dwell;
Then a sense of law and beauty
  And a face turned from the clod—
Some call it Evolution,
  And others call it God.

A haze on the far horizon,
  The infinite, tender sky,
The ripe rich tint of the cornfields,
  And the wild geese sailing high—
And all over upland and lowland
  The charm of the golden-rod—
Some of us call it Autumn
  And others call it God.

Like tides on a crescent sea-beach,
  When the moon is new and thin,

Into our hearts high yearnings
  Come welling and surging in—
Come from the mystic ocean,
  Whose rim no foot has trod,—
Some of us call it Longing,
  And others call it God.

A picket frozen on duty,
  A mother starved for her brood,
Socrates drinking the hemlock,
  And Jesus on the rood;
And millions who, humble and nameless,
  The straight, hard pathway plod,—
Some call it Consecration,
  And others call it God.

44—Letter to a Young Friend

ROBERT BURNS
(Born January 25; 1759; Died July 21, 1796)

I lang hae thought, my youthful friend,
  A something to have sent you,
Tho' it should serve nae ither end
  Than just a kind memento:
But how the subject-theme may gang,
  Let time and chance determine:
Perhaps it may turn out a sang;
  Perhaps, turn out a sermon.

Ye'll try the world soon, my lad;
  And, Andrew dear, believe me,
Ye'll find mankind an unco squad,
  And muckle they may grieve ye:
For care and trouble set your thought,
  Ev'n when your end's attained:
And a' your views may come to nought,
  Where every nerve is strained.

I'll no say, men are villains a':
   The real, harden'd wicked,
Wha hae nae check but human law,
   Are to a few res tricked;
But, och! mankind are unco weak
   An' little to be trusted;
If self the wavering balance shake,
   It's rarely right adjusted!

Yet they wha fa' in Fortune's strife,
   Their fate we should na censure;
For still, th' important end of life
   They equally may answer:
A man may hae an honest heart,
   Tho' poortith hourly stare him;
A man may tak a neebor's part,
   Yet hae nae cash to spare him.

Ay free, aff han', your story tell,
   When wi' a bosom cronie;
But still keep something to yoursel
   Ye scarcely tell to onie:
Conceal yoursel as weel's ye can
   Frae critical dissection:
But keek thro' every other man
   Wi' sharpened, sly inspection.

The sacred lowe o' weel-plac'd love,
   Luxuriantly indulge it;
But never tempt th' illicit rove,
   Tho' naething should divulge it:
I waive the quantum o' the sin.
   The hazard of concealing;
But, och! it hardens a' within,
   And petrifies the feeling!

To catch Dame Fortune's golden smile,
   Assiduous wait upon her;
And gather gear by every wile

That's justified by honour:
Not for to hide it in a hedge,
  Nor for a train-attendant;
But for the glorious privilege
  Of being independent.

The fear o' Hell's a hangman's whip
  To haud the wretch in order;
But where ye feel your honour grip,
  Let that ay be your border:
Its slightest touches, instant pause—
  Debar a' side-pretences;
And resolutely keep its laws,
  Uncaring consequences.

The great Creator to revere
  Must sure become the creature;
But still the preaching cant forbear
  And ev'n the rigid feature:
Yet ne'er with wits profane to range
  Be complaisance extended;
An atheist-laugh's a poor exchange
  For Deity offended!

When ranting round in Pleasure's ring,
  Religion may be blinded;
Or if she gie a random sting,
  It may be little minded;
But when on Life we're tempest-driv'n—
  A conscience but a canker—
A correspondence fix'd wi' Heav'n
Is sure a noble anchor!

Adieu, dear, amiable youth!
  Your heart can ne'er be wanting!
May prudence, fortitude, and truth,
  Erect your brow undaunting!
In ploughman phrase, "God send you speed,"
  Still daily to grow wiser;

And may ye better reck the rede,
  Than ever did th' adviser!

45—The Deacon's Masterpiece

or "The One-Hoss Shay"

OLIVER WENDELL HOLMES
(Born August 29, 1809; Died October 7, 1894)

Have you heard of the wonderful one-hoss shay,
That was built in such a logical way
It ran a hundred years to a day,
And then, of a sudden, it—ah, but stay,
I'll tell you what happened without delay,
Scaring the parson into fits,
Frightening people out of their wits,—
Have you heard of that, I say?

Seventeen hundred and fifty-five,
Georgius Secundus was then alive,—
Snuffy old drone from the German hive.
That was the year when Lisbon-town
Saw the earth open and gulp her down,
And Braddock's army was done so brown,
Left without a scalp to its crown.
It was on the terrible Earthquake-day
That the Deacon finished the one-hoss shay.

Now in building of chaises, I tell you what,
There is always *somewhere* a weakest spot,—
In hub, tire, felloe, in spring or thill,
In panel, or crossbar, or floor, or sill,
In screw, bolt, thoroughbrace,—lurking still,
Find it somewhere you must and will,—
Above or below, or within or without,—
And that's the reason, beyond a doubt,
A chaise *breaks down*, but doesn't *wear out*.

But the Deacon swore, (as Deacons do,
With an "I dew vum,"or an "I tell yeou,")
He would build one shay to beat the taown
'N the keounty 'n' all the kentry raoun';
It should be so built that it *couldn'* break daown:
—"Fur,"said the Deacon, "'t's mighty plain
Thut the weakes' places mus' stan' the strain;
'N the way t' fix it, uz I maintain,
Is only jest
T' make that place uz strong uz the rest."
So the Deacon inquired of the village folk
Where he could find the strongest oak,
That couldn't be split nor bent nor broke,—
That was for spokes and floor and sills;
He sent for lancewood to make the thills;
The crossbars were ash, from the straightest trees;
The panels of white-wood, that cuts like cheese,
But lasts like iron for things like these;
The hubs of logs from the "Settler's ellum,"—
Last of its timber,—they couldn't sell 'em,
Never an axe had seen their chips,
And the wedges flew from between their lips,
Their blunt ends frizzled like celery-tips;
Step and prop-iron, bolt and screw,
Spring, tire, axle, and linchpin too,
Steel of the finest, bright and blue;
Thoroughbrace bison-skin, thick and wide;
Boot, top, dasher, from tough old hide
Found in the pit when the tanner died.
That was the way he "put her through."—
"There!"said the Deacon, "naow she'll dew!"

Do! I tell you, I rather guess
She was a wonder, and nothing less!
Colts grew horses, beards turned gray,
Deacon and deaconess dropped away,
Children and grandchildren—where were they?
But there stood the stout old one-hoss shay
As fresh as on Lisbon-earthquake-day!

EIGHTEEN HUNDRED;— it came and found
The Deacon's masterpiece strong and sound.
Eighteen hundred increased by ten;—
"Hahnsum kerridge"they called it then.
Eighteen hundred and twenty came;—
Running as usual; much, the same.
Thirty and forty at last arrive,
And then come fifty, and FIFTY-FIVE.

Little of all we value here
Wakes on the morn of its hundredth year
Without both feeling and looking queer.
In fact, there's nothing that keeps its youth,
So far as I know, but a tree and truth.
(This is a moral that runs at large;
Take it. You're welcome. No extra charge.)
FIRST OF NOVEMBER,— the Earthquake- day.
There are traces of age in the one-hoss shay,
A general flavor of mild decay,
But nothing local as one may say.
There couldn't be,—for the Deacon's art
Had made it so like in every part
That there wasn't a chance for one to start.
For the wheels were just as strong as the thills,
And the floor was just as strong as the sills,
And the panels just as strong as the floor,
And the whippletree neither less nor more,
And the back-crossbar as strong as the fore,
And spring and axle and hub *encore*.
And yet, as a whole, it is past a doubt
In another hour it will be *worn out!*

First of November, Fifty-five!
This morning the parson takes a drive.
Now, small boys, get out of the way!
Here comes the wonderful one-hoss shay,
Drawn by a rat-tailed, ewe-necked bay.
"Huddup!"said the parson. Off went they.
The parson was working his Sunday's text,—

81

Had got to *fifthly*, and stopped perplexed
At what the—Moses—was coming next.
All at once the horse stood still,
Close by the meet'n'-house on the hill.
— First a shiver, and then a thrill,
Then something decidedly like a spill,—
And the parson was sitting up on a rock,
At half-past nine by the meet'n'-house clock,—
Just the hour of the Earthquake shock!
—What do you think the parson found,

When he got up and stared around?
The poor old chaise in a heap or mound,
As if it had been to the mill and ground!
You see, of course, if you're not a dunce,
How it went to pieces all at once,—
All at once, and nothing first,—
Just as bubbles do when they burst.

End of the wonderful one-hoss shay.
Logic is logic. That's all I say.

46—The Building of the Ship

HENRY WADSWORTH LONGFELLOW
(Born February 27, 1807; Died March 24, 1882)

Then the Master,
With a gesture of command,
Waved his hand;
And at the word,
Loud and sudden there was heard,
All around them and below,
The sound of hammers, blow on blow,
Knocking away the shores and spurs.
And see! She stirs!
She starts—she moves—she seems to feel
The thrill of life along her keel,
And, spurning with her foot the ground,

With one exulting, joyous bound,
She leaps into the ocean's arms!

And lo! from the assembled crowd
There rose a shout, prolonged and loud,
That to the ocean seemed to say,
"Take her, O bridegroom, old and gray,
Take her to thy protecting arms,
With all her youth and all her charms!"
How beautiful she is! How fair
She lies within those arms, that press
Her form with many a soft caress
Of tenderness and watchful care!
Sail forth into the sea, O ship!
Through wind and wave, right onward steer!
The moistened eye, the trembling lip,
Are not the signs of doubt or fear.

Sail forth into the sea of life,
O gentle, loving, trusting wife,
And safe from all adversity
Upon the bosom of that sea
Thy comings and thy goings be!
For gentleness and love and trust
Prevail o'er angry wave and gust;
And in the wreck of noble lives
Something immortal still survives!

Thou, too, sail on, O ship of State!
Sail on, O Union, strong and great!
Humanity with all its fears,
With all the hopes of future years,
Is hanging breathless on thy fate!
We know what Master laid thy keel,
What Workman wrought thy ribs of steel,
Who made each mast, and sail, and rope,
What anvils rang, what hammers beat,
In what a forge and what a heat,
Were shaped the anchors of thy hope!

Fear not each sudden sound and shock,
'Tis of the wave and not the rock;
'Tis but the flapping of the sail.
And not a rent made by the gale.
In spite of rock and tempest's roar,
In spite of false lights on the shore,
Sail on, nor fear to breast the sea!
Our hearts, our hopes, are all with thee,
Our hearts, our hopes, our prayers, our tears,
Our faith triumphant o'er our fears,
Are all with thee—are all with thee!

47—Solitude

ELLA WHEELER. WILCOX
(Born November 5, 1855; Died Oct. 30, 1919)

Laugh, and the world laughs with you;
  Weep, and you weep alone.
For the sad old earth must borrow its mirth,
  But has trouble enough of its own.
Sing, and the hills will answer;
  Sigh, it is lost on the air.
The echoes bound to a joyful sound,
  But shrink from voicing care.

Rejoice, and men will seek you;
  Grieve, and they turn and go.
They want full measure of all your pleasure,
  But they do not need your woe,
Be glad, and your friends are many;
  Be sad, and you lose them all.
There are none to decline your nectared wine,
  But alone you must drink life's gall.

Feast, and your halls are crowded;
  Fast, and the world goes by.
Succeed and give, and it helps you live,
  But no man can help you die.

There is room in the halls of pleasure
  For a long and lordly train,
But one by one we must all file on
  Through the narrow aisles of pain.

48—Knee-Deep in June

JAMES WHITCOMB RILEY
(Born October 7, 1853; Died July 22, 1916)

Tell you what I like the best—
  'Long about knee-deep in June,
'Bout the time strawberries melts
On the vine,—some afternoon
Like to jes' git out and rest,
  And not work at nothin' else!

Orchard's where I'd ruther be—
Needn't fence it in fer me!—
  Jes' the whole sky overhead,
And the whole airth underneath—
Sorto' so's a man kin breathe
  Like he on, and kindo' has
Elbow room to keerlessly
  Sprawl out len'thways on the grass
    Where the shadders thick and soft
  As the kivvers on the bed
  Mother fixes in the loft
  Allus, when they's company!
Jes' a-sorto' lazin' there—
  S'lazy, 'at you peek and peer
Through the wavin' leaves above,
Like a feller 'at's in love
  And don't know it, ner don't keer!
Everything you hear and see
  Got some sorto' interest—
  Maybe find a bluebird's nest
  Tucked up there conveenently
  Fer the boy 'at 's ap' to be

Up some other apple-tree!
Watch the swallers skootin' past
'Bout as peert as you could ast;
    Er the Bob-white raise and whiz
    Where some other's whistle is.

Ketch a shadder down below,
And look up to find the crow—
Er a hawk—away up there,
'Peerantly froze in the air!—
    Hear the old hen squawk, and squat
    Over ever' chick she's got,
Suddent-like—and she knows where
    That-air hawk is, well as you!—
    You jes' bet yer life she do!—
        Eyes a-glitterin' like glass,
        Waitin' till he makes a pass!
Pee-wees' singin', to express
    My opinion, 's second class,
Yit you'll hear 'em more er less;
    Sapsucks gittin' down to biz,
Weedin' out the lonesomeness;
    Mr. Bluejay, full o' sass,
    In them base-ball clothes o' his,
Sportin' round the orchard jes'
Like he owned the premises!
    Sun out in the fields kin sizz,
But flat on yer back, I guess,
    In the shade 's where glory is!
That's jes' what I'd like to do
Stiddy fer a year er two!

Plague! ef they ain't somepin' in
Work 'at kindo' goes ag'in
    My convictions!— 'long about
    Here in June especially!—
    Under some old apple-tree,
        Jes' a-restin' through and through,
    I could git along without

Nothin' else at all to do
Only jes' a-wishin' you
Wuz a-gittin' there like me,
And June was eternity!

Lay out there and try to see
Jes' how lazy you kin be!—
    Tumble round and souse yer head
    In the clover-bloom, er pull
    Yer straw hat acrost yer eyes
        And peek through it at the skies,
    Thinkin' of old chums 'at 's dead,
        Maybe smilin' back at you
I' betwixt the beautiful
    Clouds o' gold and white and blue!
    Month a man kin railly love—
    June, you know, I'm talkin' of!

March aint never nothin' new!—
Aprile's altogether too
    Brash fer me! and May—I jes'
    'Bominate its promises,—
Little hints o' sunshine and
Green around the timber-land—
    A few promises, and a few
    Chip-birds, and a sprout er two,—
        Drap asleep, and it turns in
        'Fore daylight and snows ag'in!—

But when June comes—Clear my throat
    With wild honey!—Rench my hair
In the dew! and hold my coat!
    Whoop out loud! and throw my hat!—
June wants me, and I'm to spare!
Spread them shadders anywhere,
I'll git down and waller there.
    And obleeged to you at that!

49—Opportunity

JOHN JAMES INGALLS
(Born December 29, 1833; Died July 16, 1900)

Master of human destinies am I.
Fame, love, and fortune on my footsteps wait,
Cities and fields I walk; I penetrate
Deserts and seas remote, and, passing by
Hovel, and mart, and palace, soon or late
I knock unbidden once at every gate!
If sleeping, wake—if feasting, rise before
I turn away. It is the hour of fate,
And they who follow me reach every state
Mortals desire, and conquer every foe
Save death; but those who doubt or hesitate,
Condemned to failure, penury and woe,
Seek me in vain and uselessly implore—
I answer not, and I return no more.

50—Wailing

JOHN BURROUGHS
(Born April 3, 1837; March 29, 1921)

Serene, I fold my hands and wait,
    Nor care for wind nor tide nor sea;
I rave no more 'gainst time or fate,
    For lo! My own shall come to me.

I stay my haste, I make delays—
    For what avails this eager pace?
I stand amid the eternal ways
    And what is mine shall know my face.

Asleep, awake, by night or day,
    The friends I seek are seeking me,
No wind can drive my bark astray
    Nor change the tide of destiny.

What matter if I stand alone?
  I wait with joy the coming years;
My heart shall reap where it has sown,
  And gamer up its fruit of tears.

The waters know their own, and draw
  The brook that springs in yonder height;
So flows the good with equal law
  Unto the soul of pure delight.

The stars come nightly to the sky;
  The tidal wave unto the sea;
Nor time, nor space, nor deep, nor high,
  Can keep my own away from me.

51—Paul Revere's Ride

HENRY WADSWORTH LONGFELLOW
(Born February 27, 1807; Died March 24, 1882)

Listen, my children, and you shall hear
Of the midnight ride of Paul Revere,
On the eighteenth of April, in Seventy-five;
Hardly a man is now alive
Who remembers that famous day and year.

He said to his friend, "If the British march
By land or sea from the town to-night,
Hang a lantern aloft in the belfry arch
Of the North Church tower as a signal light,—
One if by land, and two if by sea;
And I on the opposite shore will be,
Ready to ride and spread the alarm
Through every Middlesex village and farm,
For the country folk to be up and to arm."
Then he said "Good-night!"and with muffled oar
Silently rowed to the Charlestown shore,
Just as the moon rose over the bay,
Where swinging wide at her moorings lay

The *Somerset* British man-of-war;
A phantom ship, with each mast and spar
Across the moon like a prison bar,
And a huge black hulk, that was magnified
By its own reflection in the ride.

Meanwhile, his friend through alley and street
Wanders and watches, with eager ears,
Till in the silence around him he hears
The muster of men at the barrack door,
The sound of arms, and the tramp of feet,
And the measured tread of the grenadiers,
Marching down to their boats on the shore.

Then he climbed the tower of the Old North Church,
By the wooden stairs, with stealthy tread,
To the belfry chamber overhead,
And startled, the pigeons from their perch
On the sombre rafters, that round him made
Masses and moving shapes of shade,—
By the trembling ladder, steep and tall,
To the highest window in the wall,
Where he paused to listen and look down
A moment on the roofs of the town
And the moonlight flowing over all.

Beneath, in the churchyard, lay the dead,
In their night encampment on the hill,
Wrapped in silence so deep and still
That he could hear, like a sentinel's tread,
The watchful night-wind, as it went
Creeping along from tent to tent,
And seeming to whisper, "All is well!"
A moment only he feels the spell
Of the place and the hour, and the secret dread
Of the lonely belfry and the dead;
For suddenly all his thoughts are bent
On a shadowy something far away,
Where the river widens to meet the bay,—

A line of black that bends and floats
On the rising tide like a bridge of boats.

Meanwhile, impatient to mount and ride,
Booted and spurred, with a heavy stride
On the opposite shore walked Paul Revere.
Now he patted his horse's side,
Now he gazed at the landscape far and near,
Then, impetuous, stamped the earth,
And turned and tightened his saddle girth;
But mostly he watched with eager search
The belfry tower of the Old North Church,
As it rose above the graves on the hill,
Lonely and spectral and sombre and still.
And lo! As he looks, on the belfry's height
A glimmer, and then a gleam of light!
He springs to the saddle, the bridle he turns,
But lingers and gazes, till full on his sight
A second lamp in the belfry bums.

A hurry of hoofs in a village street,
A shape in the moonlight, a bulk in the dark,
And beneath, from the pebbles, in passing, a spark
Struck out by a steed flying fearless and fleet;
That was all! And yet, through the gloom and the light,
The fate of a nation was riding that night;
And the spark struck out by that steed, in his flight,
Kindled the land into flame with its heat.
He has left the village and mounted the steep,
And beneath him, tranquil and broad and deep,
Is the Mystic, meeting the ocean tides;
And under the alders that skirt its edge,
Now soft on the sand, now loud on the ledge,
Is heard the tramp of his steed as he rides.

It was twelve by the village clock
When he crossed the bridge into Medford town.
He heard the crowing of the cock,
And the barking of the farmer's dog,

91

And felt the damp of the river fog,
That rises after the sun goes down.

It was one by the village clock.
When he galloped into Lexington.
He saw the gilded weathercock
Swim in the moonlight as he passed,
And the meeting-house windows, black and bare,
Gaze at him with a spectral glare,
As if they already stood aghast
At the bloody work they would look upon.

It was two by the village clock,
When he came to the bridge in Concord town.
He heard the bleating of the flock,
And the twitter of birds among the trees,
And felt the breath of the morning breeze
Blowing over the meadow brown.
And one was safe and asleep in his bed
Who at the bridge would be first to fall,
Who that day would be lying dead,
Pierced by a British musket ball.

You know the rest. In the books you have read
How the British Regulars fired and fled,—
How the farmers gave them ball for ball,
From behind each fence and farmyard wall,
Chasing the redcoats down the lane,
Then crossing the fields to emerge again
Under the trees at the turn of the road,
And only pausing to fire and load.

So through the night rode Paul Revere;
And so through the night went his cry of alarm
To every Middlesex village and farm,—
A cry of defiance, and not of fear,
A voice in the darkness, a knock at the door,
And a word that shall echo for evermore!
For, borne on the night-wind of the Past,

Through all our history, to the last,
In the hour of darkness and peril and need,
The people will waken and listen to hear
The hurrying hoof-beats of that steed,
And the midnight message of Paul Revere.

52—That Time of Year

WILLIAM SHAKESPEARE
(Born April 26, 1564; Died April 23, 1616)

That time of year thou may'st in me behold
When yellow leaves, or none, or few, do hang
Upon those boughs which shake against the cold,
Bare ruin'd choirs, where late the sweet birds sang;

In me thou see'st the twilight of such day
As after sunset fadeth in the west,
Which by and by black night doth take away,
Death's second self, that seals up all in rest;
In me thou see'st the glowing of such fire
That on the ashes of his youth doth lie,
As the death-bed whereon it must expire,
Consum'd with that which it was nourish'd by:
—This thou perceiv'st, which makes thy love more
     strong,
To love that well which thou must leave ere long.

53—Plant a Tree

LUCY LARCOM
(Born March 5, 1824; Died April 17, 1893)

He who plants a tree
  Plants a hope.
  Rootlets up through fibres blindly grope;
Leaves unfold into horizons free.
  So man's life must climb

93

From the clods of time
Unto heavens sublime.
Canst thou prophesy, thou little tree,
What the glory of thy boughs shall be?

He who plants a tree
    Plants a joy;
    Plants a comfort that will never cloy;
Every day a fresh reality,
    Beautiful and strong,
    To whose shelter throng
    Creatures blithe with song.
If thou couldst but know, thou happy tree,
Of the bliss that shall inhabit thee!

He who plants a tree,—
    He plants peace.
    Under its green curtains jargons cease.
Leaf and zephyr murmur soothingly;
    Shadows soft with sleep
    Down tired eyelids creep,
    Balm of slumber deep.
Never hast thou dreamed, thou blessed tree,
Of the benediction thou shalt be.

He who plants a tree,—
    He plants youth;
    Vigor won for centuries in sooth;
Life of time, that hints eternity!
    Boughs their strength uprear;
    New shoots, every year,
    On old growths appear;
Thou shalt teach the ages, sturdy tree,
Youth of soul is immortality.

He who plants a tree,—
    He plants love,
    Tents of coolness spreading out above
Wayfarers he may not live to see.

Gifts that grow are best;
Hands that bless are blest;
Plant! life does the rest!
Heaven and earth help him who plants a tree,
And his work its own reward shall be.

54—Abou Ben Adhem

JAMES HENRY LEIGH HUNT
(Born October 29, 1784; Died August 28, 1859)

Abou Ben Adhem (may his tribe increase!)
Awoke one night from a deep dream of peace,
And saw, within the moonlight in his room,
Making it rich, and like a lily in bloom,
An Angel writing in a book of gold:
Exceeding peace had made Ben Adhem bold,
And to the Presence in the room he said,
"What writest thou?" The Vision raised its head,
And with a look made of all sweet accord
Answered, "The names of those who love the Lord,"
"And is mine one?" said Abou. "Nay, not so,"
Replied the Angel, Abou spoke more low,
But cheerly still; and said, "I pray thee, then,
Write me as one that loves his fellow-men."

The Angel wrote, and vanished. The next night
It came again with a great wakening light,
And showed the names whom love of God had blessed,
And, lo! Ben Adhem's name led all the rest!

55—The Bells

EDGAR ALLAN POE
(Born January 19, 1809; Died October 7, 1849)

Hear the sledges with the bells—
Silver bells!
What a world of merriment their melody foretells!
How they tinkle, tinkle, tinkle,
In the icy air of night!
While the stars that oversprinkle
All the heavens, seem to twinkle
With a crystalline delight;
Keeping time, time, time,
In a sort of Runic rhyme,
To the tintinnabulation that so musically wells
From the bells, bells, bells, bells,
Bells, bells, bells,—
From the jingling and the tinkling of the bells.

Hear the mellow wedding bells.
Golden bells!
What a world of happiness their harmony foretells!
Through the balmy air of night
How they ring out their delight!
From the molten-golden notes,
And all in tune,
What a liquid ditty floats
To the turtle dove that listens, while she gloats
On the moon!
Oh, from out the sounding cells,
What a gush of euphony voluminously wells!
How it swells!
How it dwells
On the Future! How it tells
Of the rapture that impels
To the swinging and the ringing
Of the bells, bells, bells,

Of the bells, bells, bells, bells,
Bells, bells, bells—
To the rhyming and the chiming of the bells!

Hear the loud alarm bells—
Brazen bells!
What a tale of terror now their turbulency tells!
In the startled ear of night
How they scream out their affright!
Too much horrified to speak
They can only shriek, shriek,
Out of tune,
In a clamorous appealing to the mercy of the fire,
In a mad expostulation with the deaf and frantic fire,
Leaping higher, higher, higher,
With a desperate desire,
And a resolute endeavor,
Now—now to sit or never,
By the side of the pale-faced moon.
Oh, the bells, bells, bells!
What a tale their terror tells
Of despair!
How they clang, and clash, and roar!
What a horror they outpour
On the bosom of the palpitating air!
Yet the ear it fully knows,
By the twanging,
And the clanging,
How the danger ebbs and flows;
Yet the ear distinctly tells,
In the jangling,
And the wrangling,
How the danger sinks and swells,
By the sinking or the swelling in the anger of the bell
Of the bells—
Of the bells, bells, bells, bells,
Bells, bells, bells—
In the clamor and the clangor of the bells!

97

Hear the tolling of the bells
Iron bells!
What a world of solemn thought their monody compels
In the silence of the night,
How we shiver with affright
At the melancholy menace of their tone!
For every sound that floats
From the rust within their throats
Is a groan.
And the people—ah, the people—
They that dwell up in the steeple,
All alone,
And who tolling, tolling, tolling,
In that muffled monotone,
Feel a glory in so rolling
On the human heart a stone—
They are neither man nor woman—
They are neither brute nor human—
They are Ghouls:
And their king it is who tolls;
And he rolls, rolls, rolls,
Rolls
A paean from the bells!
And his merry bosom swells
With the paean of the bells!
And he dances, and he yells;
Keeping time, time, time,
In a sort of Runic rhyme,
To the paean of the bells—
Of the bells:
Keeping time, time, time,
In a sort of Runic rhyme,
To the throbbing of the bells—
Of the bells, bells, bells—
To the sobbing of the bells;
Keeping time, time, time,
As he knells, knells, knells,
In a happy Runic rhyme,
To the rolling of the bells—

Of the bells, bells, bells—
To the tolling of the bells,
Of the bells, bells, bells, bells—
Bells, bells, bells—
To the moaning and the groaning of the bells!

56—Elegy Written in a Country Church-Yard

THOMAS GRAY
(Born December 26, 1716; Died July 30, 1771)

The curfew tolls the knell of parting day,
  The lowing herd winds slowly o'er the lea,
The ploughman homeward plods his weary way,
  And leaves the world to darkness and to me.

Now fades the glimmering landscape on the sight,
  And all the air a solemn stillness holds,
Save where the beetle wheels his droning flight,
  And drowsy tinklings lull the distant folds;
Save that, from yonder ivy-mantled tower,
  The moping owl does to the moon complain
Of such as, wandering near her secret bower,
  Molest her ancient, solitary reign.

Beneath those rugged elms, that yew-tree's shade,
  Where heaves the turf in many a mould'ring heap,
Each in his narrow cell forever laid,
  The rude forefathers of the hamlet sleep.

The breezy call of incense-breathing mom,
  The swallow twittering from the straw-built shed,
The cock's shrill clarion, or the echoing horn,
  No more shall rouse them from their lowly bed.

For them no more the blazing hearth shall burn,
  Or busy housewife ply her evening care;
No children run to lisp their sire's return,

   Or climb his knees the envied kiss to share.

Oft did the harvest to their sickle yield,
   Their furrow oft the stubborn glebe has broke;
How jocund did they drive their team afield!
   How bowed the woods beneath their sturdy stroke!

Let not ambition mock their useful toil,
   Their homely joys, and destiny obscure;
Nor grandeur hear with a disdainful smile
   The short and simple annals of the poor.

The boast of heraldry, the pomp of power,
   And all that beauty, all that wealth e'er gave,
Awaits alike the inevitable hour:
   The paths of glory lead but to the grave.

Nor you, ye proud, impute to these the fault,
   If memory o'er their tomb no trophies raise
Where through the long-drawn aisle and fretted vault
   The pealing anthem swells the note of praise.

Can storied urn or animated bust
   Back to its mansion call the fleeting breath?
Can Honor's voice provoke the silent dust,
   Or Flattery soothe the dull cold ear of Death?

Perhaps in this neglected spot is laid
   Some heart once pregnant with celestial fire;
Hands that the rod of empire might have swayed,
   Or wak'd to ecstasy the living lyre;

But Knowledge to their eyes her ample page,
   Rich with the spoils of time, did ne'er unroll;
Chill Penury repressed their noble rage,
   And froze the genial current of the soul.

Full many a gem of purest ray serene
   The dark, unfathomed caves of ocean bear:

Full many a flower is bom to blush unseen,
   And waste its sweetness on the desert air.

Some village Hampden, that, with dauntless breast
   The little tyrant of his fields withstood,
Some mute, inglorious Milton, here may rest;
   Some Cromwell guiltless of his country's blood.

The applause of listening senates to command,
   The threats of pain and ruin to despise,
To scatter plenty o'er a smiling land,
   And read their history in a nation's eyes.

Their lot forbade: nor circumscribed alone
   Their growing virtues, but their crimes confined;
Forbade to wade thro' slaughter to a throne,
   And shut the gates of mercy on mankind.

The struggling pangs of conscious truth to hide,
   To quench the blushes of ingenuous shame,
Or heap the shrine of Luxury and Pride
   With incense kindled at the Muse's flame.

Far from the madding crowd's ignoble strife,
   "Their sober wishes never learned to stray;
Along the cool sequestered vale of life
   They kept the noiseless tenor of their way.

Yet even these bones from insult to protect,
   Some frail memorial still erected nigh,
With uncouth rhymes and shapeless sculpture decked,
   Implores the passing tribute of a sigh.

Their name, their years, spelt by the unlettered Muse,
   The place of fame and elegy supply:
And many a holy text around she strews
   That teach the rustic moralist to die.

For who, to dumb forgetfulness a prey,
   This pleasing anxious being e'er resigned,
Left the warm precincts of the cheerful day,
   Nor cast one longing, lingering look behind?

On some fond breast the parting soul relies,
   Some pious drops the closing eye requires;
Ev'n from the tomb the voice of Nature cries,
   Ev'n in our ashes live their wonted fires.

For thee who, mindful of the unhonor'd dead,
   Dost in these lines their artless tale relate;
If chance, by lonely contemplation led,
   Some kindred spirit shall inquire thy fate,—

Haply some hoary-headed swain may say:
   "Oft have we seen him, at the peep of dawn,
Brushing with hasty steps the dews away,
   To meet the sun upon the upland lawn.

"There at the foot of yonder nodding beech,
   That wreathes its old fantastic roots so high,
His listless length at noontide would he stretch,
   And pore upon the brook that babbles by.

"Hard by yon wood, now smiling as in scorn,
   Mutt'ring his wayward fancies, he would rove;
Now drooping, woeful-wan, like one forlorn,
   Or craz'd with care, or crossed in hopeless love.

"One morn I missed him on the custom'd hill,
   Along the heath, and near his favorite tree;
Another came,—nor yet beside the rill,
   Nor up the lawn, nor at the wood was he:

"The next, with dirges due, in sad array,
   Slow through the church-way path we saw him borne;
Approach and read (for thou canst read) the lay
   Grav'd on the stone beneath yon aged thorn."

THE EPITAPH

Here rests his head upon the lap of earth,
    A youth to fortune and to fame unknown;

Fair Science frown'd not on his humble birth,
    And Melancholy mark'd him for her own.

Large was his bounty, and his soul sincere;
    Heaven did a recompense as largely send:
He gave to misery all he had, a tear;
    He gained from heaven(twas all he wished) a friend.

No farther seek his merits to disclose,
    Or draw his frailties from their dread abode,—
(There they alike in trembling hope repose,)
    The bosom of his Father and his God.

57—Cuddle Doon

ALEXANDER ANDERSON
(Born April 30, 1845; Died July 11, 1909)

The bairnies cuddle doon at nicht
    Wi' muckle fash an' din.
"Oh, try and sleep, ye waukrife rogues;
    Your faither's comin' in."
They never heed a word I speak.
    I try to gie a froon;
But aye I hap them up, an' cry,
    "Oh, bairnies, cuddle doon!"

Wee Jamie wi' the curly held—
    He aye sleeps next the wa'—
Bangs up an' cries, "I want a piece"
    The rascal starts them a'.
I rin an' fetch them pieces, drinks—

103

They stop a wee the soun'—
Then draw the blankets up, an' cry,
   "Noo, weanies, cuddle doon!"

But ere five minutes gang, wee Rab
   Cries oot, frae 'neath the claes,
Mither, mak' Tam gie ower at ance:
   He's kittlin' wi' his taes."
The mischiefs in that Tam for tricks;
   He'd bother half the toon.
But aye I hap them up, an' cry,
   "Oh, baitnies, cuddle doon!"

At length they hear their father's fit;
   An', as he steeks the door,
They turn their faces to the wa',
   While Tam pretends to snore.
"Hae a' the weans been gude?"he asks,
   As he pits aff his shoon.
"The bairnies, John, are in their beds,
   An' lang since cuddled doon."

An' just afore we bed oorsels,
   We look at oor wee lambs.
Tam has his airm roun' wee Rab's neck,
   An' Rab his airm roun'. Tam's.
I lift wee Jamie up the bed,
   An' as I straik each croon,
I whisper, till my heart fills up,
   "Oh, bairnies, cuddle doon!"

The bairnies cuddle doon at nicht
   Wi' mirth that's dear to me;
But soon the big warl's cark an' care
   Will quaten doon their glee.
Yet, come what will to ilka ane,
   May He who rules aboon
Aye whisper, though their pows be bald,
   "Oh, bairnies, cuddle doon!"

58—Sonnet on His Blindness

JOHN MILTON
(Born December 9, 1608; Died November 8, 1674)

When I consider how my light is spent
  Ere half my days, in this dark world and wide,
  And that one talent, which is death to hide,
Lodged with me useless, though my soul more bent
To serve therewith my Maker, and present
  My true account, lest He, returning, chide:
  "Doth God exact day labor, light denied?"
I fondly ask; but Patience, to prevent
  That murmur, soon replies, "God doth not need
    Either man's work, or His own gifts; who best
    Bear His mild yoke, they serve Him best.
      His state
Is kingly. Thousands at His bidding speed,
  And post o'er land and ocean without rest;
    They also serve who only stand and wait,"

59—Thanatopsis

WILLIAM CULLEN BRYANT
(Born November 3, 1794; Died June 12, 1878)

To him who, in the love of Nature, holds
Communion with her visible forms, she speaks
A various language: for his gayer hours
She has a voice of gladness, and a smile
And eloquence of beauty; and she glides
Into his darker musings, with a mild
And healing sympathy, that steals away
Their sharpness, ere he is aware. When thoughts
Of the last bitter hour come like a blight
Over thy spirit, and sad images

105

Of the stern agony, and shroud, and pall,
And breathless darkness, and the narrow house,
Make thee to shudder, and grow sick at heart,—
Go forth under the open sky, and list
To Nature's teachings, while from all around—
Earth and her waters, and the depths of air—
Comes a still voice;—Yet a few days, and thee
The all-beholding sun shall see no more
In all his course; nor yet in the cold ground,
Where thy pale form was laid, with many tears,
Nor in the embrace of ocean, shall exist
Thy image. Earth, that nourished thee, shall claim
Thy growth, to be resolved to earth again;
And, lost each human trace, surrendering up
Thine individual being, shalt thou go
To mix forever with the elements;
To be a brother to the insensible rock,
And to the sluggish clod, which the rude swain
Turns with his share, and treads upon. The oak
Shall send his roots abroad, and pierce thy mold.
Yet not to thine eternal resting place
Shalt thou retire alone—nor couldst thou wish
Couch more magnificent. Thou shalt lie down
With patriarchs of the infant world—with kings,
The powerful of the earth—the wise, the good,
Fair forms, and hoary seers of ages past,
All in one mighty sepulcher. The hills,
Rock-ribbed, and ancient as the sun; the vales
Stretching in pensive quietness between;
The venerable woods; rivers that move
In majesty, and the complaining brooks,
That make the meadows green; and, poured round all,
Old ocean's gray and melancholy waste—
Are but the solemn decorations all
Of the great tomb of man! The golden sun,
The planets, all the infinite host of heaven,
Are shining on the sad abodes of death,
Through the still lapse of ages. All that tread
The globe are but a handful to the tribes

That slumber in its bosom. Take the wings
Of morning, pierce the Barcan wilderness,
Or lose thyself in the continuous woods
Where rolls the Oregon and hears no sound
Save his own dashings—yet the dead are there;
And millions in those solitudes, since first
The flight of years began, have laid them down
In their last sleep—the dead reign there alone!
So shalt thou rest, and what if thou withdraw
In silence from the living; and no friend
Take note of thy departure? All that breathe
Will share thy destiny. The gay will laugh
When thou art gone, the solemn brood of care
Plod on, and each one as before shall chase
His favorite phantom; yet all these shall leave
Their mirth and their employments, and shall come
And make their bed with thee. As the long train
Of ages glides away, the sons of men—
The youth in life's green spring, and he who goes
In the full strength of years, matron and maid,
And the sweet babe, and the gray-headed man—
Shall one by one be gathered to thy side,
By those, who in their turn shall follow them.

So live that when thy summons comes to join
The innumerable caravan that moves
To that mysterious realm, where each shall take
His chamber in the silent halls of death,
Thou go not, like the quarry-slave at night,
Scourged to his dungeon, but, sustained and soothed
By an unfaltering trust, approach thy grave
Like one who wraps the drapery of his couch
About him, and lies down to pleasant dreams.

60—The Children's Hour

HENRY WADSWORTH LONGFELLOW
(Born February 27, 1807; Died March 24, 1882)

Between the dark and the daylight,
  When the light is beginning to lower,
Conies a pause in the day's occupations
  That is known as the Children's Hour.

I hear in the chamber above me
  The patter of little feet,
The sound of a door that is opened,
  And voices soft and sweet.

From my study I see in the lamplight,
  Descending the broad hall stair,
Grave Alice and laughing Allegra,
  And Edith with golden hair.

A whisper, and then a silence;
  Yet I know by their merry eyes,
They are plotting and planning together
  To take me by surprise.

A sudden rush from the stairway,
  A sudden raid from the hall!
By three doors left unguarded
  They enter my castle wall!

They climb up into my turret,
  O'er the arms and back of my chair;
If I try to escape, they surround me;
  They seem to be everywhere.

They almost devour me with kisses,
  Their arms about me entwine,
Till I think of the Bishop of Bingen
  In his Mouse-Tower on the Rhine.

Do you think, O blue-eyed banditti,
　Because you have scaled the wall,
Such an old mustache as I am
　Is not a match for you all?

I have you fast in my fortress,
　And will not let you depart,
But put you down into the dungeon
　In the round-tower of my heart.

And there will I keep you forever,
　Yes, forever and a day,
Till the wall shall crumble to ruin,
　And moulder in dust away.

61—Invictus

WILLIAM ERNEST HENLEY
(Born August 23, 1849; Died July 12, 1903)

Out of the night that covers me,
　Black as the Pit from pole to pole,
I thank whatever gods may be
　For my unconquerable soul.

In the fell clutch of circumstance
　I have not winced nor cried aloud.
Under the bludgeonings of chance
　My head is bloody, but unbowed.

Beyond this place of wrath and tears
　Looms but the horror of the shade,
And yet the menace of the years
　Finds, and shall find me, unafraid.

It matters not how strait the gate,
　How charged with punishments the scroll,
I am the master of my fate;
　I am the captain of my soul.

62—The Owl and the Pussy-Cat

EDWARD LEAK

(Born May 12, 1812; Died January 30, 1888)

The Owl and the Pussy-Cat went to sea
  In a beautiful pea-green boat.
They took some honey and plenty of money
  Wrapped up in a five-pound note.
The Owl looked up to the stars above,
  And sang to a small guitar,
"O lovely Pussy! O Pussy, my love!
  What a beautiful Pussy you are,—
    You are;
What a beautiful Pussy you are!"

Pussy said to the Owl, "You elegant fowl,
  How charmingly sweet you sing!
Oh, let us be married,—too long we have tarried,—
  But what shall we do for a ring?"
They sailed away for a year and a day,
  To the land where the bong-tree grows;
And there, in a wood, a Piggy-wig stood,—
  With a ring at the end of his nose,
    His nose;
  With a ring at the end of his nose.

"Dear Pig, are you willing to sell for one shilling
  Your ring?"Said the Piggy, "I will."
So they took it away, and were married next day
  By the Turkey who lives on the hill.
They dined upon mince and slices of quince,
  Which they ate with a runcible spoon;
And hand in hand, on the edge of the sand,
  They danced by the light of the moon,—
    The moon;
  They danced by the light of the moon.

63—Horatius

THOMAS BABINGTON MACAULAY
(Born October 25, 1800; Died December 28, 1859)

Lars Porsena of Clusium,
  By the nine gods he swore
That the great house of Tarquin
  Should suffer wrong no more.
By the nine gods he swore it,
  And named a trysting day,
And bade his messengers ride forth,
East and west and south and north,
  To summon his array.

East and west and south and north
  The messengers ride fast,
And tower and town and cottage
  Have heard the trumpet's blast.
The horsemen and the footmen.
  Are pouring in amain
From many a stately market-place,
From many a fruitful plain;

And now hath every city
  Sent up her tale of men;
The foot are fourscore thousand
  The horse are thousands ten.
Before the gates of Sutrium
  Is met the great array,
A proud man was Lars Porsena
  Upon the trysting day.

But by the yellow Tiber
  Was tumult and affright:
From all the spacious champagne
  To Rome men took their flight.
A mile around the city,
  The throng stopped up the ways;

A fearful sight it was to see
  Through two long nights and days.

Now, from the rock Tarpeian,
  Could the wan burghers spy
The line of blazing villages
  Red in the midnight sky.
The Fathers of the City,
  They sat all night and day
For every hour some horseman came
  With tidings of dismay.

They held a council standing
  Before the river-gate;
Short time was there, ye well may guess,
  For musing or debate.
Outspake the Consul roundly:
  "The bridge must straight go down;
For since Janiculum is lost
  Naught else can save the town."

Just then a scout came flying,
  All wild with haste and fear:
"To arms! to arms! Sir Consul;
  Lars Porsena is here."
On the low hills to westward
  The Consul fixed his eye,
And saw the swarthy storm of dust
  Rise fast along the sky.

And nearer, fast and nearer,
  Doth the red whirlwind come;
And louder still and still more loud,
From underneath that rolling cloud,
Is heard the trumpet's war-note proud,
  The trampling and the hum.
And plainly and more plainly
  Now through the gloom appears,
Far to left and far to right,

In broken gleams of dark-blue light,
The long array of helmets bright,
  The long array of spears.

But the Consul's brow was sad,
  And the Consul's speech was low,
And darkly looked he at the wall,
  And darkly at the foe:
"Their van will be upon us
  Before the bridge goes down;
And if they once may win the bridge
  What hope to save the town?"

Then outspake brave Horatius,
  The captain of the gate:
"To every man upon this earth
  Death cometh soon or late.
And how can man die better
  Than facing fearful odds
For the ashes of his fathers
  And the temples of his gods?
"Hew down the bridge, Sir Consul,
  With all the speed ye may;
I, with two more to help me,
  Will hold the foe in play,—
In yon strait path a thousand
  May well be stopped by three.
Now who will stand on either hand,
  And keep the bridge with me?"

Then outspake Spurius Lartius,—
  A Ramnian proud was he:
"Lo, I will stand at thy right hand,
  And keep the bridge with thee."
And outspake strong Herminius,—
  Of Titian blood was he:
"I will abide on thy left side,
  And keep the bridge with thee."

"Horatius,"quoth the Consul,
  "As thou sayest, so let it be."
And straight against that great array,
  Forth went the dauntless Three.
Now, while the Three were tightening
  Their harness on their backs,
The Consul was the foremost man
  To take in hand an axe;
And Fathers mixed with Commons
  Seized hatchet, bar, and crow,
And smote upon the planks above,
  And loosed the props below.

Meanwhile the Tuscan army,
  Right glorious to behold,
Came flashing back the noonday light,
Rank behind rank, like surges bright
  Of a broad sea of gold.
Four hundred trumpets sounded
  A peal of warlike glee,
As that great host, with measured tread,
And ensigns spread.
Rolled slowly towards the bridge's head,
  Where stood the dauntless Three.

The three stood calm and silent,
  And looked upon the foes,
And a great shout of laughter
  From all the vanguard rose;
And forth three chiefs came spurring
  Before that mighty mass;
To earth they sprang, their swords they drew,
And lifted high their shields, and flew
  To win the narrow pass,

Aunus, from green Tifernum,
  Lord of the hill of vines;
And Seius, whose eight hundred slaves
  Sicken in Ilva's mines;

114

And Picus, long to Clusium
　Vassal in peace and war.

Stout Lartius hurled down Aunus
　Into the stream beneath;
Herminius struck at Seius,
　And clove him to the teeth;
At Picus brave Horatius
　Darted one fiery thrust,
And the proud Umbrian's gilded arms
　Clashed in the bloody dust.

But now no sound of laughter
　Was heard amongst the foes.
A wild and wrathful clamor
　From all the vanguard rose.
Six spears' lengths from the entrance
　Halted that mighty mass,
And for a space no man came forth
　To win the narrow pass.

But, hark! the cry is Astur:
　And lo! the ranks divide;
And the great lord of Luna
　Comes with his stately stride.
Upon his ample shoulders
　Clangs loud the fourfold shield,
And in his hand he shakes the brand
　Which none but he can wield.

He smiled on those bold Romans,
　A smile serene and high;
He eyed the flinching Tuscans,
　And scorn was in his eye.
Quoth he, "The she-wolfs litter
　Stand savagely at bay;
But will ye dare to follow,
　If Astur clears the way?"

115

Then, whirling up his broadsword
   With both hands to the height,
He rushed against Horatius,
   And smote with all his might,
With shield and blade Horatius
   Right deftly turned the blow,
The blow, though turned, came yet too nigh;
It missed his helm, but gashed his thigh.
The Tuscans raised a joyful cry
   To see the red blood flow.

He reeled, and on Herminius
   He leaned one breathing-space,
Then, like a wild-cat mad with wounds,
   Sprang right at Astur's face.
Through teeth and skull and helmet
   So fierce a thrust he sped,
The good sword stood a handbreadth out
   Behind the Tuscan's head.

And the great lord of Luna
   Fell at that deadly stroke,
As falls on Mount Avernus
   A thunder-smitten oak.
Far o'er the crashing forest
   The giant arms lie spread;
And the pale augurs, muttering low,
   Gaze on the blasted head.

On Astur's throat Horatius
   Right firmly pressed his heel,
And thrice and four times tugged amain,
   Ere he wrenched out the steel.
"And see,"he cried, "the welcome,
   Fair guests, that waits you here!
What noble Lucumo comes next
   To taste our Roman cheer?"

But meanwhile axe and lever
  Have manfully been plied,
And now the bridge hangs tottering
  Above the boiling tide.
"Come back, come back, Horatius!"
  Loud cried the Fathers all;
"Back, Lartius! back, Herminius!
  Back, ere the ruin fall!"

Back darted Spurius Lartius;
  Herminius darted back;
And, as they passed, beneath their feet
  They felt the timbers crack;
But when they turned their faces,
  And on the further shore
Saw brave Horatius stand alone,
  They would have crossed once more.

But, with a crash like thunder,
  Fell every loosened beam,
And, like a dam, the mighty wreck
  Lay right athwart the stream;
And a long shout of triumph
  Rose from the walls of Rome.
As to the highest turret-tops
  Was splashed the yellow foam.

Alone stood brave Horatius,
  But constant still in mind,—
Thrice thirty thousand foes before,
  And the broad flood behind.
"Down with him!"cried false Sextus,
  With a smile on his pale face;
"Now yield thee,"cried Lars Porsena,
  "Now yield thee to our grace!"

Round turned he, as not deigning
  Those craven ranks to see;
Naught spake he to Lars Porsena,

To Sextus naught spake he;
But he saw on Palatinus
  The white porch of his home;
And he spake to the noble river
  That rolls by the towers of Rome:

"O Tiber! Father Tiber!
  To whom the Romans pray
A Roman's life, a Roman's arms,
  Take thou in charge this day!"
So he spake, and, speaking, sheathed
  The good sword by his side,
And, with his harness on his back,
  Plunged headlong in the tide.

No sound of joy or sorrow
  Was heard from either bank,
But friends and foes in dumb surprise,
With parted lips and straining eyes,
  Stood gazing where he sank;
And when above the surges
  They saw his crest appear,
All Rome sent forth a rapturous cry,
And even the ranks of Tuscany
  Could scarce forbear to cheer.

But fiercely ran the current,
  Swollen high by months of rain,
And fast his blood was flowing;
  And he was sore in pain,
And heavy with his armor,
  And spent with changing blows;
And oft they thought him sinking,
  But still again he rose.

And now he feels the bottom;—
  Now on dry earth he stands;
Now round him throng the Fathers
  To press his gory hands.

And, now, with shouts and clapping,
  And noise of weeping loud,
He enters through the River Gate,
  Borne by the joyous crowd.

64—She Walks in Beauty

GEORGE GORDON BYRON
(Born January 22, 1788; Died April 19, 1824)

She walks in beauty, like the night
  Of cloudless climes and starry skies,
And all that's best of dark and bright
  Meet in her aspect and her eyes,
Thus mellowed to that tender light
  Which heaven to gaudy day denies.

One shade the more, one ray the less
  Had half impaired the nameless grace
Which waves in every raven tress,
  Or softly lightens o'er her face,
Where thoughts serenely sweet express
  How pure, how dear their dwelling-place.

And on that cheek, and o'er that brow,
  So soft, so calm, yet eloquent,
The smiles that win, the tints that glow
  But tell of days in goodness spent—
A mind at peace with all below,
  A heart whose love is innocent.

65—The Eternal Goodness

JOHN GREENLEAF WHITTIER
(Born December 17, 1807; Died September 7, 1892)

O friends! with whom my feet have trod
  The quiet aisles of prayer,

Glad witness to your zeal for God
   And love of man I bear,

I trace your lines of argument;
   Your logic linked and strong
I weigh as one who dreads dissent,
   And fears a doubt as wrong.

But still my human hands are weak
   To hold your iron creeds:
Against the words ye bid me speak
   My heart within me pleads.

Who fathoms the Eternal Thought?
   Who talks of scheme and plan?
The Lord is God! He needeth not
   The poor device of man.

I walk with bare, hushed feet the ground
   Ye tread with boldness shod;
I dare not fix with mete and bound
   The love and power of God.

Ye praise His justice; even such
   His pitying love I deem:
Ye seek a king; I fain would touch
   The robe that hath no seam.

Ye see the curse which overbroods
   A world of pain and loss;
I hear our Lord's beatitudes
   And prayer upon the cross.

More than your schoolmen teach, within
   Myself, alas! I know:
Too dark ye cannot paint the sin,
   Too small the merit show.

I bow my forehead to the dust,
  I veil mine eyes for shame,
And urge, in trembling self-distrust,
  A prayer without a claim.

I see the wrong that round me lies,
  I feel the guilt within;
I hear, with groan and travail-cries,
  The world confess its sin.

Yet, in the maddening maze of things,
  And tossed by storm and flood,
To one fixed trust my spirit clings;
  I know that God is good!

Not mine to look where cherubim
  And seraphs may not see,
But nothing can be good in Him
  Which evil is in me.

The wrong that pains my soul below
  I dare not throne above,
I know not of His hate,—I know
  His goodness and His love.

I dimly guess from blessings known
  Of greater out of sight,
And, with the chastened Psalmist, own
  His judgments too are right.

I long for household voices gone,
  For vanished smiles I long,
But God hath led my dear ones on,
  And He can do no wrong.

I know not what the future hath
  Of marvel or surprise,
Assured alone that life and death
  His mercy underlies.

And if my heart and flesh are weak
   To bear an untried pain,
The bruised reed He will not break,
   But strengthen and sustain.

No offering of my own I have,
   Nor works my faith to prove;
I can but give the gifts He gave,
   And plead His love for love.

And so beside the Silent Sea
   I wait the muffled oar;
No harm from Him can come to me
   On ocean or on shore,

I know not where His islands lift
   Their fronded palms in air;
I only know I cannot drift
   Beyond His love and care.

O brothers! if my faith is vain,
   If hopes like these betray,
Pray for me that my feet may gain
   The sure and safer way.

And Thou, O Lord! by whom are seen
   Thy creatures as they be,
Forgive me if too close I lean
   My human heart on Thee!

66—Perseverance

JOHANN WOLFGANG VON GOETHE
(Born August 28, 1749; Died March 22, 1832)

We must not hope to be mowers,
   And to gather the ripe gold ears,
Unless we have first been sowers
   And watered the furrows with tears.

It is not just as we take it,
  This mystical world of ours,
Life's field will yield as we make it
  A harvest of thorns or of flowers.

67—If

RUDYARD KIPLING
(Born December 30, 1865; Died January 18, 1936)

If you can keep your head when all about you
  Are losing theirs and blaming it on you;
If you can trust yourself when all men doubt you,
  But make allowance for their doubting too:
If you can wait and not be tired by waiting,
  Or, being lied about, don't deal in lies,
Or being hated don't give way to hating,
  And yet don't look too good, nor talk too wise;

If you can dream—and not make dreams your master;
  If you can think—and not make thoughts your aim,
If you can meet with Triumph and Disaster
  And treat those two impostors just the same:
If you can bear to hear the truth you've spoken
  Twisted by knaves to make a trap for fools,
Or watch the things you gave your life to, broken,
  And stoop and build 'em up with worn-out tools;

If you can make one heap of all your winnings
  And risk it on one turn of pitch-and-toss,
And lose, and start again at your beginnings,
  And never breathe a word about your loss:
If you can force your heart and nerve and sinew
  To serve your turn long after they are gone,
And so hold on when there is nothing in you
  Except the Will which says to them: "Hold on!"

If you can talk with crowds and keep your virtue,

Or walk with Kings—nor lose the common touch,
If neither foes nor loving friends can hurt you,
  If all men count with you, but none too much:
If you can fill the unforgiving minute
  With sixty seconds' worth of distance run,
Yours is the Earth and everything that's in it,
  And—which is more—you'll be a Man, my, son!

68—The Day is Done

HENRY WADSWORTH LONGFELLOW
(Born February 27, 1807; Died March 24, 1882)

The day is done, and the darkness
  Falls from the wings of Night,
As a feather is wafted downward
  From an eagle in his flight.

I see the lights of the village
  Gleam through the rain and the mist,
And a feeling of sadness comes o'er me.
  That my soul cannot resist:

A feeling of sadness and longing,
  That is not akin to pain,
And resembles sorrow only
  As the mist resembles the rain.

Come, read to me some poem,
  Some simple and heartfelt lay,
That shall soothe this restless feeling,
  And banish the thoughts of day.

Not from the grand old masters,
  Not from the bards sublime,
Whose distant footsteps echo
  Through the corridors of Time.

For, like strains of martial music,
  Their mighty thoughts suggest
Life's endless toil and endeavor;
  And tonight I long for rest.

Read from some humbler poet,
  Whose songs gushed from his heart,
As showers from the clouds of summer,
  Or tears from the eyelids start;

Who, through long days of labor,
  And nights devoid of ease,
Still heard in his soul the music
  Of wonderful melodies.

Such songs have power to quiet
  The restless pulse of care,
And come like the benediction
  That follows after prayer.

Then read from the treasured volume
  The poem of thy choice,
And lend to the rhyme of the poet
  The beauty of thy voice.

And the night shall be filled with music
  And the cares, that infest the day,
Shall fold their tents, like the Arabs,
  And as silently steal away.

69—Love of Country

From "The Lay of the Last Minstrel"

SIR WALTER SCOTT
(Born August 15, 1771; Died September 21, 1832)

Breathes there the man with soul so dead
Who never to himself hath said:

125

"This is my own, my native land?"
Whose heart hath ne'er within him burned
As home his footsteps he hath turned,
   From wandering on a foreign strand?
If such there breathe, go mark him well;
For him no minstrel raptures swell;
High though his titles, proud his name,
Boundless his wealth as wish can claim,
Despite those titles, power and pelf,
The wretch concentred all in self,
Living, shall forfeit fair renown,
And, doubly dying, shall go down
To the vile dust from whence he sprung,
Unwept, unhonored, and unsung.

70—Nobility

ALICE CARY
(Born April 26, 1820; Died February 12, 1871)

True worth is in being, not *seeming*,—
   In doing, each day that goes by,
Some little good—not in dreaming
   Of great things to do by and by.
For whatever men say in their blindness,
   And spite of the fancies of youth,
There's nothing so kingly as kindness,
   And nothing so royal as truth.

We get back our mete as we measure—
   We cannot do wrong and feel right,
Nor can we give pain and gain pleasure,
   For justice avenges each slight.
The air for the wing of the sparrow,
   The bush for the robin and wren,

But always the path that is narrow
　And straight, for the children of men.

'Tis not in the pages of story
　The heart of its ills to beguile,
Though he who makes courtship to glory
　Gives all that he hath for her smile.
For when from her heights he has won her,
　Alas! It is only to prove
That nothing's so sacred as honor,
　And nothing so loyal as love!

We cannot make bargains for blisses,
　Nor catch them like fishes in nets;
And sometimes the thing our life misses
　Helps more than the thing which it gets.
For good lieth not in pursuing,
　Nor gaining of great nor of small,
But just in the doing, and doing
　As we would be done by, is all.

Through envy, through malice, through hating,
　Against the world, early and late,
No jot of our courage abating—
　Our part is to work and to wait.
And slight is the sting of his trouble
　Whose winnings are less than his worth;
For he who is honest is noble,
　Whatever his fortunes or birth.

71—The Minuet

MARY MAPES DODGE
(Born January 26, 1838; Died August 21, 1905)

Grandma told me all about it,
Told me so I couldn't doubt it,
How she danced, my grandma danced; long ago—
How she held her pretty head,

How her dainty skirt she spread,
How she slowly leaned and rose—long ago.

Grandma's hair was bright and sunny,
Dimpled cheeks, too, oh, how funny!
Really quite a pretty girl—long ago.
Bless her! why, she wears a cap,
Grandma does, and takes a nap
Every single day: and yet
Grandma danced the minuet—long ago.

"Modern ways are quite alarming,"
Grandma says, "but boys were charming"
(Girls and boys she means, of course) "long ago."
Brave but modest, grandly shy;
She would like to have us try
Just to feel like those who met
In the graceful minuet—long ago.

72—Childe Harold's Farewell to England

GEORGE GORDON BYRON
(Born January 22, 1788; Died April 19, 1824)

Adieu, adieu! my native shore
  Fades o'er the waters blue;
The night-winds sigh, the breakers roar,
  And shrieks the wild sea-mew.
Yon sun that sets upon the sea,
  We follow in his flight;
Farewell awhile to him and thee,
  My native land—Good-night.

A few short hours and he will rise
  To give the morrow birth;
And I shall hail the main and skies,
  But not my mother earth.
Deserted is my own good hall,
  Its hearth is desolate;

Wild weeds are gathering on the wall;
 My dog howls at the gate.

Come hither, hither, my little page!
 Why dost thou weep and wail?
Or dost thou dread the billow's rage,
 Or tremble at the gale?
But dash the tear-drop from thine eye;
 Our ship is swift and strong;
Our fleetest falcon scarce can fly
 More merrily along.

"Let winds be shrill, let waves roll high,
 I fear not wave nor wind:
Yet marvel not. Sir Childe, that I
 Am sorrowful in mind;
For I have from my father gone,
 A mother whom I love,
And have no friends, save these alone,
 But thee—and One above.

"My father blessed me fervently,
 Yet did not much complain;
But sorely will my mother sigh
 Till I come back again."—
Enough, enough, my little lad!
 Such tears become thine eye;
If I thy guileless bosom had,
 Mine own would not be dry.

73—God Save the Flag

OLIVER WENDELL HOLMES
(Born August 29, 1809; Died October 7, 1894)

Washed in the blood of the brave and the blooming,
 Snatched from the altars of insolent foes,
Burning with star-fires, but never consuming,
 Flash its broad ribbons of lily and rose.

Vainly the prophets of Baal would rend it,
  Vainly his worshippers pray for its fall;
Thousands have died for it, millions defend it,
  Emblem of justice and mercy to all:

Justice that reddens the sky with her terrors,
  Mercy that comes with her white-handed train,
Soothing all passions, redeeming all errors,
  Sheathing the sabre and breaking the chain.

Borne on the deluge of old usurpations,
  Drifted our Ark o'er the desolate seas,
Bearing the rainbow of hope to the nations,
  Tom from the storm-cloud and flung to the breeze!

God bless the Flag and its loyal defenders,
  While its broad folds o'er the battle-field wave,
Till the dim star-wreath rekindle its splendors,
  Washed from its stains in the blood of the brave!

74—The Raven

EDGAR ALLAN POE
(Born January 19, 2809; Died October 7, 1849)

Once upon a midnight dreary, while I pondered, weak and weary,
  Over many a quaint and curious volume of forgotten lore,
While I nodded, nearly napping, suddenly there came a tapping,
  As of some one gently rapping, rapping at my chamber door.
  " 'Tis some visitor," I muttered, "tapping at my chamber door;
    Only this, and nothing more."

Ah, distinctly I remember, it was in the bleak December,
  And each separate dying ember wrought its ghost upon the floor.
Eagerly I wished the morrow; vainly I had sought to borrow
  From my books surcease of sorrow, sorrow for the lost Lenore,
  For the rare and radiant maiden whom the angels name Lenore,
    Nameless here forevermore.

And the silken sad uncertain rustling of each purple curtain
   Thrilled me—filled me with fantastic terrors never felt before;
So that now, to still the beating of my heart, I stood repeating,
   " 'Tis some visitor entreating entrance at my chamber door.
   Some late visitor entreating entrance at my chamber door;
      This it is, and nothing more."

Presently my soul grew stronger; hesitating then no longer,
   "Sir," said I, "or madam, truly your forgiveness I implore;
But the fact is, I was napping, and so gently you came rapping,
   And so faintly you came tapping, tapping at my chamber door,
   That I scarce was sure I heard you." Here I opened wide the door;—
      Darkness there, and nothing more.

Deep into the darkness peering, long I stood there, wondering, fearing,
   Doubting, dreaming dreams no mortals ever dared to dream before;
But the silence was unbroken, and the stillness gave no token,
   And the only word there spoken was the whispered word, "Lenore?"
   This I whispered, and an echo murmured back the word, "Lenore!"
      Merely this, and nothing more.

Back into the chamber turning, all my soul within me burning,
   Soon again I heard a tapping, something louder than before,
"Surely," said I, "surely, that is something at my window lattice;
   Let me see, then, what thereat is, and this mystery explore;
   Let my heart be still a moment, and this mystery explore;
      'Tis the wind, and nothing more."

Open here I flung the shutter, when, with many a flirt and flutter.
   In there stepped a stately raven, of the saintly days of yore.
Not the least obeisance made he; not a minute stopped or stayed he;
   But with mien of lord or lady, perched above my chamber door;
   Perched upon a bust of Pallas, just above my chamber door,
      Perched, and sat, and nothing more.

Then this ebony bird beguiling my sad fancy into smiling,
   By the grave and stem decorum of the countenance it wore,
"Though thy crest be shorn and shaven, thou," I said, "art sure no craven,

131

Ghastly, grim, and ancient raven, wandering from the nightly shore.
   Tell me what thy lordly name is on the Night's Plutonian shore."
         Quoth the raven, "Nevermore."

Much I marveled this ungainly fowl to hear discourse so plainly,
   Though its answer little meaning, little relevancy bore;
For we cannot help agreeing that no living human being
   Ever yet was blessed with seeing bird above his chamber door,
   Bird or beast upon the sculptured bust above his chamber door,
         With such name as "Nevermore."

But the raven, sitting lonely on that placid bust, spoke only
   That one word, as if his soul in that one word he did outpour.
Nothing further then he uttered; not a feather then he fluttered;
   Till I scarcely more than muttered, "Other friends have flown before;
   On the morrow *he* will leave me, as my hopes have flown before."
         Then the bird said, "Nevermore."

Startled at the stillness broken by reply so aptly spoken,
   "Doubtless," said I, "what it matters is its only stock and store,
Caught from some unhappy master, whom unmerciful disaster
   Followed fast and followed faster, till his songs one burden bore,—
   Till the dirges of his hope that melancholy burden bore
         Of "Never—nevermore."

But the raven still beguiling all my fancy into smiling,
   Straight I wheeled a cushioned seat in front of bird and bust and door;
Then, upon the velvet sinking, I betook myself to linking
   Fancy unto fancy, thinking what this ominous bird of yore,
What this grim, ungainly, ghastly, gaunt, and ominous bird of yore
         Meant in croaking, :Nevermore."

This I sat engaged in guessing, but no syllable expressing
   To the fowl, whose fiery eyes now burned into my bosom's core;
This and more I sat divining, with my head at ease reclining
   On the cushion's velvet lining that the lamplight gloated o'er,
   But whose velvet violet lining with the lamplight gloating o'er
         She shall press, ah, nevermore!

Then, methought, the air grew denser, perfumed from an unseen censer
  Swung by seraphim whose footfalls tinkled on the tufted floor.
"Wretch" I cried, "thy God hath lent thee—by these angels
    he hath sent thee
  Respite-respite and nepenthe from thy memories of Lenore!
  Quaff, O quaff this kind nepenthe, and forget this lost Lenore!"
    Quoth the raven, "Nevermore!"

"Prophet!" said I, "thing of evil!—prophet still, if bird or devil!
  Whether tempter sent, or whether tempest tossed thee here ashore.
Desolate, yet all undaunted, on this desert land enchanted,—
  On this home by horror haunted—tell me truly, I implore:
  Is there—*is* there balm in Gilead?—tell me—tell me Iimplore!"
    Quoth the raven, "Nevermore."

"Prophet!" said I, "thing of evil—prophet still, if bird or devil!
  By that heaven that bends above us—by that God we both adore—
Tell this soul with sorrow laden, if, within the distant Aidenn,
  It shall clasp a sainted maiden, whom the angels name Lenore—
  Clasp a rare and radiant maiden, whom the angels name Lenore?"
    Quoth the raven, "Nevermore."

"Be that word our sign of parting, bird or fiend!" I shrieked, upstarting—
  "Get thee back into the tempest and the Night's Plutonian shore!
Leave no black plume as a token of that lie thy soul hath spoken!
  Leave my loneliness unbroken!—quit the bust above my door!
  Take thy beak from out my heart, and take thy form from off my door!"
    Quoth the raven, "Nevermore."

And the raven, never flitting, still is sitting, still is sitting
  On the pallid bust of Pallas just above my chamber door;
And his eyes have all the seeming of a demon's that is dreaming;
  And the lamplight o'er him streaming throws the shadow on the floor;
  And my soul from out that shadow that lies floating on the floor
    Shall be lifted—nevermore!

75—The Highwayman

ALFRED NOYES
(Born September 16, 1880; Died June 25, 1958)

PART ONE

The wind was a torrent of darkness among the gusty trees,
The moon was a ghostly galleon tossed upon cloudy seas,
The road was a ribbon of moonlight over the purple moor,
    And the highwayman came riding,
    Riding, riding,
The highwayman came riding, up to the old inn-door.

He'd a French cocked-hat on his forehead, a bunch of lace at his chin,
A coat of the claret velvet, and breeches of brown doeskin;
They fitted with never a wrinkle: his boots were up to the thigh!
    And he rode with a jeweled twinkle,
    His pistol butts a-twinkle.
His rapier hilt a-twinkle, under the jeweled sky.

Over the cobbles he clattered and clashed in the dark inn-yard,
And he tapped with his whip on the shutters, but all was locked and barred;
He whistled a tune to the window, and who should be waiting there
    But the landlord's black-eyed daughter,
    Bess, the landlord's daughter,
Plaiting a dark red love-knot into her long black hair.

And dark in the dark old inn-yard a stable-wicket creaked
Where Tim the ostler listened; his face was white and peaked;
His eyes were hollows of madness, his hair like mouldy hay,
    But he loved the landlord's daughter,
    The landlord's red-lipped daughter,
Dumb as a dog he listened, and he heard the robber say:

"One kiss, my bonny sweetheart, I'm after a prize tonight,
But I shall be back with the yellow gold before the morning light;
Yet, if they press me sharply, and harry me through the day,

Then look for me by moonlight,
        Watch for me by moonlight,
I'll come to thee by moonlight, though hell should bar the way."

He rose upright in the stirrups; he scarce could reach her hand,
But she loosened her hair i' the casement! His face burnt like a brand
As the black cascade of perfume came tumbling over his breast;
        And he kissed its waves in the moonlight,
        (Oh, sweet black waves in the moonlight!)
Then he tugged at his rein in the moonlight, and galloped away to the West.

PART TWO

He did not come in the dawning: he did not come at noon;
And out o' the tawny sunset, before the rise o' the moon,
When the road was a gypsy's ribbon, looping the purple moor,
        A red-coat troop came marching,
        Marching, marching,
King George's men came marching, up to the old inn-door.
They said no word to the landlord, they drank his ale instead.

But they gagged his daughter and bound her to the foot of her narrow bed;
Two of them knelt at her casement, with muskets at their side!
        There was death at every window;
        And hell at one dark window;
For Bess could see, through her casement, the road that *he* would ride.

   They had tied her up to attention, with many a sniggering jest;
They had bound a musket beside her, with the barrel beneath her breast!
"Now keep good watch!"and they kissed her.
She heard the dead man say—
        Look for me by moonlight;
        Watch for me by moonlight;
I'll come to thee by moonlight, though hell should bar the way!
She twisted her hands behind her; but all the knots held good!
She writhed her hands till her fingers were wet with sweat or blood!
They stretched and strained in the darkness, and the hours crawled
    by like years,

135

Till, now, on the stroke of midnight,
Cold, on the stroke of midnight,
The tip of one finger touched it!
The trigger at least was hers!
The tip of one finger touched it; she strove no more for the rest!
Up, she stood up to attention, with the barrel beneath her breast,
She would not risk their hearing! she would not strive again;
For the road lay bare in the moonlight,
Blank and bare in the moonlight;
And the blood of her veins in the moonlight throbbed to her love's refrain.

Tlot-tlot; tlot-tlot! Had they heard it? The horse-hoofs ringing clear;
Tlot-tlot, tlot-tlot, in the distance? Were they deaf that they did not hear?
Down the ribbon of moonlight, over the brow of the hill,
The highwayman came riding,
Riding, riding!
The red-coats looked to their priming! She stood up straight and still!

Tlot-tlot, in the frosty silence! *Tlot-tlot,* in the echoing night!
Nearer he came and nearer! Her face was like a light!
Her eyes grew wide for a moment! she drew one last deep breath,
Then her finger moved in the moonlight,
Her musket shattered the moonlight,
Shattered her breast in the moonlight and warned him—
with her death.

He turned; he spurred to the West; he did not know she stood
Bowed, with her head o'er the musket, drenched with her own red blood!
Not till the dawn he heard it, his face grew grey to hear
How Bess, the landlord's daughter,
The landlord's black-eyed daughter,
Had watched for her love in the moonlight, and died in the darkness there.

Back, he spurred like a madman, shrieking a curse to the sky,
With the white road smoking behind him and his rapier brandished high!
Blood-red were his spurs i' the golden noon; wine-red was his velvet coat,
When they shot him down on the highway,
Down like a dog on the highway,
And he lay in his blood on the highway, with the bunch of lace at his throat.

And still of a winter's night, they say, when the wind is in the trees,
When the moon is a ghostly galleon tossed upon cloudy seas,
When the road is a ribbon of moonlight over the purple moor,
    A highwayman comes riding,
    Riding, riding,
A highwayman comes riding, up to the old inn-door.

Over the cobbles he clatters and clangs in the dark inn-yard;
He taps with his whip on the shutters, but all is locked and barred;
He whistles a tune to the window, and who should be waiting there
    But the landlord's black-eyed daughter,
    Bess, the landlord's daughter,
Plaiting a dark red love-knot into her long black hair.

76—A Psalm of Life

HENRY WADSWORTH LONGFELLOW
(Born February 27, 1807; Died March 24, 1882)

Tell me not, in mournful numbers,
  Life is but an empty dream!—
For the soul is dead that slumbers,
  And things are not what they seem.

Life is real! Life is earnest!
  And the grave is not its goal;
Dust thou art, to dust returnest,
  Was not spoken of the soul.

Not enjoyment, and not sorrow,
  Is our destined end or way;
But to act, that each tomorrow
  Find us farther than today.

Art is long, and Time is fleeting,
  And our hearts, though stout and brave,
Still, like muffled drums, are beating
  Funeral marches to the grave.

In the world's broad field of battle,
  In the bivouac of life,
Be not like dumb, driven cattle!
  Be a hero in the strife!

Trust no Future, howe'er pleasant!
  Let the dead Past bury its dead!
Act,—act in the living Present!
  Heart within, and God o'erhead!

Lives of great men all remind us
  We can make our lives sublime,
And, departing, leave behind us
  Footprints on the sands of time.

Footprints, that perhaps another,
  Sailing o'er life's solemn main,
A forlorn and shipwrecked brother,
  Seeing, shall take heart again.

Let us then be up and doing,
  With a heart for any fate;
Still achieving, still pursuing,
  Learn to labor and to wait.

77—For A' That and A' That

ROBERT BURNS
(Born January 25, 1759; Died July 21, 1796)

Is there for honest poverty
That hings his head, and a' that?
The coward slave, we pass him by;
We dare be poor for a' that!
For a' that, and a' that,
Our toils obscure, and a' that;
The rank is but the guinea stamp
The man's the gowd for a' that!

What tho' on hamely fare we dine,
Wear hodden gray, and a' that?
Gie fools their silks, and knaves their wine
A man's a man for a' that!
For a' that, and a' that,
Their tinsel show, and a' that;
The honest man, though e'er sae poor,
Is king o'' men, for a' that!

Ye see yon birkie ca'd a lord,
Wha struts, an' stares, an' a' that
Tho' hundreds worship at his word,
He's but a coof for a' that;
For a' that, and a' that,
His riband, star, and a' that;
The man of independent mind,
He looks an' laughs at a' that.

A prince can make a belted knight,
A marquis, duke, and a' that;
But an honest man's aboon his might—
Gude faith, he mauna fa' that!
For a' that, and a' that,
Their dignities, an' a' that;
The pith o' sense, and pride o' worth,
Are higher rank than a' that.

Then let us pray that come it may,
As come it will for a' that,
That sense and worth, o'er a' the earth,
May bear the gree, an' a' that.
For a' that, and a' that,
It's comin' yet, for a' that—
That man to man, the warld o'er,
Shall brithers be for a' that.

78—Jest 'Fore Christmas

EUGENE FIELD
(Born September 3, 1850; Died November 4, 1895)

Father calls me William, sister calls me Will,
Mother calls me Willie, but the fellers call me Bill!
Mighty glad I ain't a girl—ruther be a boy,
Without them sashes, curls, an' things that's worn by Fauntleroy!
Love to chawnk green apples an' go swimmin' in the lake—
Hate to take the castor-ile they give for belly-ache!
Most all the time, the whole year round, there ain't no flies on me,
But jest 'fore Christmas I'm as good as I kin be!

Got a yeller dog named Sport, sick him on the cat;
First thing she knows she doesn't know where she is at!
Got a clipper sled, an' when us kids goes out to slide,
'Long comes the grocery cart, an' we all hook a ride!
But sometimes when the grocery man is worrited an' cross,
He reaches at us with his whip, an' larrups up his hoss.
An' then I laff an' holler, "Oh, ye never teched *me!*"
But jest 'fore Christmas I'm as good as I kin be!

Gran'ma says she hopes that when I git to be a man,
I'll be a missionarer like her oldest brother, Dan,
As was et up by the cannibuls that live in Ceylon's Isle,
Where every prospeck pleases, an' only man is vile!
But gran'ma she has never been to see a Wild West show,
Nor read the life of Daniel Boone, or else I guess she'd know
That Buff'lo Bill an' cowboys is good enough for me!
Excep' jest 'fore Christmas, when I'm as good as I kin be!

And then old Sport he hangs around, so solemn-like an' still,
His eyes they seem a-sayin': "What's the matter, little Bill?"
The old cat sneaks down off her perch an' wonders what's become
Of them two enemies of hern that used to make things hum!
But I am so perlite an' tend so earnestly to biz.
That mother says to father: "How improved our Willie is!"
But father, havin' been a boy hisself, suspicions me
When, jest 'fore Christmas, I'm as good as I kin be!

For Christmas, with its lots an' lots of candies, cakes, an toys,
Was made, they say, for proper kids an' not for naughty boys;
So wash yer face an' bresh yer hair, an' mind yer p's and q's.
And don't bust out yer pantaloons, and don't wear out yer shoes;
Say "Yessum" to the ladies, and "Yessur" to the men,
An' when they's company, don't pass yer plate for pie again;
But, thinkin' of the things yer'd like to see upon that tree,
Jest 'fore Christmas be as good as yer kin be!

79—Gradatim

JOSIAH GILBERT HOLLAND
(Born July 24, 1819; Died October 12, 1881)

Heaven is not gained at a single bound;
  But we build the ladder by which we rise
  From the lowly earth to the vaulted skies,
And we mount to its summit round by round.

I count this thing to be grandly true,
  That a noble deed is a step toward God—
  Lifting the soul from the common sod
To a purer air and a broader view.

We rise by things that are 'neath our feet;
  By what we have mastered of good and gain;
  By the pride deposed and the passion slain,
And the vanquished ills that we hourly meet.

We hope, we aspire, we resolve, we trust,
  When the morning calls us to life and light,
  But our hearts grow weary, and, ere the night,
Our lives are trailing the sordid dust.

We hope, we resolve, we aspire, we pray,
  And we think that we mount the air on wings
  Beyond the recall of sensual things,
While our feet still cling to the heavy clay.

141

Wings for the angels, but feet for men!
  We may borrow the wings to find the way—
  We may hope, and resolve, and aspire, and pray,
But our feet must rise, or we fall again.

Only in dreams is a ladder thrown
  From the weary earth to the sapphire walls;
  But the dream departs, and the vision falls,
And the sleeper wakes on his pillow of stone.

Heaven is not reached at a single bound:
  But we build the ladder by which we rise
  From the lowly earth to the vaulted skies,
And we mount to its summit round by round.

80—The Barefoot Boy

JOHN GREENLEAF WHITTIER
(Born December 17, 1807; Died September 7, 1892)

Blessings on thee, little man,
Barefoot boy, with cheek of tan!
With thy turned-up pantaloons,
And thy merry whistled tunes;
With thy red lip, redder still,
Kissed by strawberries on the hill;
With the sunshine on thy face,
Through thy torn brim's jaunty grace,
From my heart I give thee joy,—
I was once a barefoot boy.
Prince thou art,— the grown-up man
Only is republican,
Let the million-dollared ride!
Barefoot, trudging at his side,
Thou hast more than he can buy,
In the reach of ear and eye—
Outward sunshine, inward joy;
Blessings on thee, barefoot boy!

Oh, for boyhood's painless play,
Sleep that wakes in laughing day,
Health that mocks the doctor's rules,
Knowledge never learned of schools,
Of the wild bee's morning chase,
Of the wild flower's time and place,
Flight of fowl and habitude
Of the tenants of the wood;
How the tortoise bears his shell,
How the woodchuck digs his cell,
And the groundmole sinks his well;
How the robin feeds her young,
How the oriole's nest is hung,
Where the whitest lilies blow,
Where the freshest berries grow,
Where the ground-nut trails its vine,
Where the wood-grape's clusters shine,

Of the black wasp's cunning way,—
Mason of his walls of clay,—
And the architectural plans
Of gray-hornet artisans!—
For, eschewing books and tasks,
Nature answers all he asks,
Hand in hand with her he walks,
Face to face with her he talks,
Part and parcel of her joy,—
Blessings on the barefoot boy!

Oh, for boyhood's time of June,
Crowding years in one brief moon,
When all things I heard or saw,
Me, their master, waited for.
I was rich in flowers and trees,
Humming-birds and honeybees;
For my sport the squirrel played,
Plied the snouted mole his spade;
For my task the blackberry cone

Purpled over hedge and stone;
Laughed the brook for my delight
Through the day and through the night,—
Whispering at the garden wall,
Talked with me from fall to fall;
Mine the sand-rimmed pickerel pond,
Mine the walnut slopes beyond,
Mine, on bending orchard trees,
Apples of Hesperides!
Still, as my horizon grew,
Larger grew my riches too;
All the world I saw or knew
Seemed a complex Chinese toy
Fashioned for a barefoot boy.

Oh, for festal dainties spread,
Like my bowl of milk and bread,
Pewter spoon and bowl of wood,
On the doorstone, gray and rude!
O'er me, like a regal tent,
Cloudy-ribbed, the sunset bent,
Purple-curtained, fringed with gold,
Looped in many a wind-swung fold,
While for music came the play
Of the pied frog's orchestra,
And, to light the noisy choir,
Lit the fly his lamp of fire.
I was monarch: pomp and joy
Waited on thee, barefoot boy!

Cheerily, then, my little man,
Live and laugh as boyhood can!
Though the flinty slopes be hard,
Stubble-speared the new-mown sward,
Every morn shall lead thee through
Fresh baptisms of the dew;
Every evening from thy feet
Shall the cool wind kiss the heat;
All too soon these feet must hide

In the prison cells of pride,
Lose the freedom of the sod,
Like a colt's for work be shod,
Made to tread the mills of toil,
Up and down in ceaseless moil;
Happy if their track be found;
Never on forbidden ground;
Happy if they sink not in
Quick and treacherous sands of sin,
Ah! that thou couldst know thy joy,
Ere it passes, barefoot boy!

81—Polonius' Advice to Laertes

WILLIAM SHAKESPEARE
(Born April 23 (?), 1564; Died April 23, 1616)

There,—my blessing with you!
And these few precepts in thy memory
See thou character.—Give thy thoughts no tongue,
Nor any unproportion'd thought his act.
Be thou familiar, but by no means vulgar.
The friends thou hast, and their adoption tried,
Grapple them to thy soul with hoops of steel;
But do not dull thy palm with entertainment
Of each new-hatched, unfledged comrade. Beware
Of entrance to a quarrel; but being in,
Bear't that the opposed may, beware of thee.
Give every man thine ear, but few thy voice:
Take each man's censure, but reserve thy judgment.
Costly thy habit as thy purse can buy,
But not expressed in fancy; rich, not gaudy:
For the apparel oft proclaims the man.
Neither a borrower nor a lender be,
For loan oft loses both itself and friend,
And borrowing dulls the edge of husbandry,
This above all: to thine own self be true,
And it must follow, as the night the day,
Thou canst not then be false to any man.

145

82—The Flag Goes By

HENRY HOLCOMB BENNETT
(Born December 5, 1863; Died April 30, 1924)

Hats off!
Along the street there comes
A blare of bugles, a ruffle of drums,
A flash of color beneath the sky:
Hats off!
The flag is passing by!

Blue and crimson and white it shines,
Over the steel-tipped, ordered lines.
Hats off!
The colors before us fly;
But more than the flag is passing by.

Sea-fights and land-fights, grim and great,
Fought to make and to save the State:
Weary marches and sinking ships;
Cheers of victory on dying lips;

Days of plenty and years of peace;
March of a strong land's swift increase;
Equal justice, right and law,
Stately honor and reverend awe;

Sign of a nation, great and strong
To ward her people from foreign wrong:
Pride and glory and honor,—all
Live in the colors to stand or fall.

Hats off!
Along the street there comes
A blare of bugles, a ruffle of drums;

And loyal hearts are beating high:
Hats off!
The flag is passing by!

83—"The Things That Are More Excellent"

WILLIAM WATSON
(Born August 2, 1858; August 13, 1935)

As we wax older on this earth,
   Till many a toy that charmed us seems
Emptied of beauty, stripped of worth,
   And mean as dust and dead as dreams,—
For gauds that perished, shows that passed,
   Some recompense the Fates have sent:
Thrice lovelier shine the things that last,
   The things that are more excellent.

Tired of the Senate's barren brawl,
   An hour with silence we prefer,
Where statelier rise the woods than all
   Yon towers of talk at Westminster.
Let this man prate and that man plot,
   On fame or place or title bent:
The votes of veering crowds are not
   The things that are more excellent.

Shall we perturb and vex our soul
   For "wrongs" which no true freedom mar,
Which no man's upright walk control,
   And from no guiltless deed debar?
What odds though tonguesters heal, or leave
   Unhealed, the grievance they invent?
To things, not phantoms, let us cleave—
   The things that are more excellent.

Nought nobler is, than to be free:
   The stars of heaven are free because

147

In amplitude of liberty
   Their joy is to obey the laws.
From servitude to freedom's *name*
   Free thou thy mind in bondage pent;
Depose the fetich, and proclaim
   The things that are more excellent.

And in appropriate dust be hurled
   That dull, punctilious god, whom they
That call their tiny clan the world,
   Serve and obsequiously obey:
Who con their ritual of Routine,
   With minds to one dead likeness blent,
And never ev'n in dreams have seen
   The things that are more excellent.

To dress, to call, to dine, to break
   No canon of the social code,
The little laws that lacqueys make,
   The futile decalogue of Mode,—
How many a soul for these things lives,
   With pious passion, grave intent!
While Nature careless-handed gives
   The things that are more excellent.

To hug the wealth ye cannot use,
   And lack the riches all may gain,—
O blind and wanting wit to choose,
   Who house the chaff and burn the grain!
And still doth life with starry towers
   Lure to the bright, divine ascent!—
Be yours the things ye would: be ours
   The things that are more excellent.

The grace of friendship— mind and heart
   Linked with their fellow heart and mind;
The gains of science, gifts of art;
   The sense of oneness with our kind;
The thirst to know and understand—

A large and liberal discontent:
These are the goods in life's rich hand,
   The things that are more excellent.

In faultless rhythm the ocean rolls,
   A rapturous silence thrills the skies;
And on this earth are lovely souls,
   That softly look with aidful eyes.
Though dark, O God, Thy course and track,
   I think Thou must at least have meant
That nought which lives should wholly lack
   The things that are more excellent.

84—Concord Hymn

RALPH WALDO EMERSON
(Born May 25, 1803; Died April 27, 1882)

By the rude bridge that arched the flood,
   Their flag to April's breeze unfurled,
Here once the embattled farmers stood,
And fired the shot heard round the world.

The foe long since in silence slept;
   Alike the conqueror silent sleeps;
And Time the ruined bridge has swept
   Down the dark stream which seaward creeps.

On this green bank, by this soft stream,
   We set today a votive stone;
That memory may their deed redeem,
   When, like our sires, our sons are gone.

Spirit, that made those spirits dare
   To die, and leave their children free,
Bid Time and Nature gently spare
   The shaft we raise to them and thee.

85—Keep a-Goin'

FRANK L. STANTON
(Born February 22, 1857; Died January 7, 1927)

If you strike a thorn or rose,
    Keep a-goin'!
If it hails or if it snows,
    Keep a-goin'!
'Taint no use to sit an' whine
When the fish ain't on your line;
Bait your hook an' keep a-tryin'—
    Keep a-goin'!

When the weather kills your crop,
    Keep a-goin'!
Though 'tis work to reach the top,
    Keep a-goin'!
S'pose you're out o' ev'ry dime,
Gittin' broke ain't any crime;
Tell the world you're feelin' *prime*—
    Keep a-goin'!

When it looks like all is up,
    Keep a-goin'!
Drain the sweetness from the cup,
    Keep a-goin'!
See the wild birds on the wing,
Hear the bells that sweetly ring,
When you feel like singin', sing—
    Keep a-goin'!

86—Life Sculpture

GEORGE WASHINGTON DOANE
(Born May 27, 1799; Died April 27, 1859)

Chisel in hand stood a sculptor boy
  With his marble block before him,
And his eyes lit up with a smile of joy,
  As an angel-dream passed o'er him.

He carved the dream on that shapeless stone,
  With many a sharp incision;
With heaven's own light the sculpture shone, —
  He'd caught that angel-vision.

Children of life are we, as we stand
  With our lives uncarved before us,
Waiting the hour when, at God's command,
  Our life-dream shall pass o'er us.

If we carve it then on the yielding stone,
  With many a sharp incision,
Its heavenly beauty shall be our own,—
  Our lives, that angel-vision.

87—The Choir Invisible

GEORGE ELIOT (MARY ANN EVANS)
(Born November 22, 1819; Died December 22, 1880)

Oh, may I join the choir invisible
Of those immortal dead who live again
In minds made better by their presence; live
In pulses stirred to generosity,
In deeds of daring rectitude, in scorn
For miserable aims that end with self,
In thoughts sublime that pierce the night like stars,
And with their mild persistence urge men's search
To vaster issues. So to live is heaven:

151

To make undying music in the world,
Breathing a beauteous order that controls
With growing sway the growing life of man.
So we inherit that sweet purity
For which we struggled, failed, and agonized
With widening retrospect that bred despair.
Rebellious flesh that would not be subdued,
A vicious parent shaming still its child,
Poor anxious penitence, is quick dissolved;
Its discords, quenched by meeting harmonies,
Die in the large and charitable air,
And all our rarer, better, truer self
That sobbed religiously in yearning song,
That watched to ease the burden of the world,
Laboriously tracing what must be,
And what may yet be better,—saw within
A worthier image for the sanctuary,
And shaped it forth before the multitude,
Divinely human, raising worship so
To higher reverence more mixed with love, —
That better self shall live till human Time
Shall fold its eyelids, and the human sky
Be gathered like a scroll within the tomb
Unread forever. This is life to come, —
Which martyred men have made more glorious
For us who strive to follow. May I reach
That purest heaven,—be to other souls
The cup of strength in some great agony,
Enkindle generous ardor, feed pure love,
Beget the smiles that have no cruelty,
Be the sweet presence of a good diffused,
And in diffusion ever more intense!
So shall I join the choir invisible
Whose music is the gladness of the world.

88—Marmion and Douglas

From "Marmion"

SIR WALTER SCOTT
(Born August 15, 1771; Died September 21, 1832)

The train from out the castle drew,
But Marmion stopped to bid adieu: —
  "Though something I might plain," he said,
"Of cold respect to stranger guest,
Sent hither by your king's behest,
  While in Tantallon's towers I stayed,
Part we in friendship from your land,
And, noble Earl, receive my hand." —
But Douglas round him drew his cloak,
Folded his arms, and thus he spoke: —
"My manors, halls, and bowers shall still
Be open, at my sovereign's will,
To each one whom he lists, howe'er
Unmeet to be the owner's peer.
My castles are my king's alone
From turret to foundation-stone,
The hand of Douglas is his own;
And never shall in friendly grasp
The hand of such as marmion clasp." —

Burned Marmion's swarthy cheek like fire,
And shook his very frame for ire,
  And—"This to me!" he said, —
"An't were not for thy hoary beard,
Such hand as Marmion's had not spared
  To cleave the Douglas' head!
And first I tell thee, haughty Peer,
He who does England's message here,
Although the meanest in her state,
May well, proud Angus, be thy mate:
And, Douglas, more I tell thee here,
  Even in thy pitch of pride,
Here in thy hold, thy vassals near,

153

(Nay, never look upon your lord,
And lay your hands upon your sword,)
   I tell thee, thou'rt defied!
And if thou said'st I am not peer
To any lord in Scotland here,
Lowland or Highland, far or near,
   Lord Angus, thou hast lied!" —
On the Earl's cheek the flush of rage
O'ercame the ashen hue of age;
Fierce he broke forth, —"And dar'st thou then
To beard the lion in his den,
   The Douglas in his hall?
And hop'st thou hence unscathed to go?
No, by St. Bride of Bothwell, no!
Up drawbridge, grooms—what, Warder, ho!
   Let the portcullis fall." —

Lord Marmion turned,—well was his need!—
And dashed the rowels in his steed,
Like arrow through the archway sprung;
The ponderous gate behind him rung:
To pass there was such scanty room,
The bars, descending, razed his plume.

The steed along the drawbridge flies,
Just as it trembled on the rise;
Not lighter does the swallow skim
Along the smooth lake's level brim;
And when Lord Marmion reached his band
He halts, and turns with clenched hand,
And shout of loud defiance pours,
And shook his gauntlet at the towers.

89—Ode on a Grecian Urn

JOHN KEATS
(Born October 31, 1795; Died February 23, 1821)

Thou still unravished bride of quietness,
  Thou foster child of silence and slow time,
Sylvan historian, who canst thus express
  A flowery tale more sweetly than our rhyme:
What leaf-fring'd legend haunts about thy shape
  Of deities or mortals, or of both,
In Tempe or the dales of Arcady?
  What men or gods are these? What maidens loath?
What mad pursuit? What struggle to escape?
  What pipes and timbrels? What wild ecstasy?

Heard melodies are sweet, but those unheard
  Are sweeter; therefore, ye soft pipes, play on;
Not to the sensual ear, but, more endeared,
  Pipe to the spirit ditties of no tone.
Fair youth, beneath the trees, thou canst not leave
  Thy song, nor ever can those trees be bare;
    Bold Lover, never, never canst thou kiss,
Though winning near the goal—yet, do not grieve;
  She cannot fade, though thou hast not thy bliss
    Forever wilt thou love, and she be fair!

Ah, happy, happy boughs! that cannot shed
  Your leaves, nor ever bid the Spring adieu;
And, happy melodist, unwearièd,
  Forever piping songs forever new;
More happy love! more happy, happy love!
  Forever warm and still to be enjoyed,
    Forever panting, and forever young;
All breathing human passion far above,
  That leaves a heart high-sorrowful and cloyed,
    A burning forehead, and a parching tongue.

Who are these coming to the sacrifice?
  To what green altar, O mysterious priest,

155

Lead'st thou that heifer lowing at the skies,
　　And all her silken flanks with garlands dressed?
What little town by river or sea shore,
　　Or mountain-built with peaceful citadel,
　　　Is emptied of this folk, this pious morn?
And, little town, thy streets for evermore
　　Will silent be; and not a soul to tell
　　　Why thou art desolate, can e'er return.

O Attic shape! Fair attitude! with brede
　　Of marble men and maidens overwrought,
With forest branches and the trodden weed;
　　Thou, silent form, dost tease us out of thought
As doth eternity. Cold Pastoral!
　　When old age shall this generation waste,
　　　Thou shalt remain, in midst of other woe
Than ours, a friend to man, to whom thou say'st,
　　"Beauty is truth, truth beauty"—that is all
　　　Ye know on earth, and all ye need to know.

90—The Heart of the Tree

HENRY CUYLER BUNNER
(Born August 3, 1855; Died May 11, 1896)

WHAT does he plant who plants a tree?
He plants a friend of sun and sky;
He plants the flag of breezes free;
The shaft of beauty, towering high.
He plants a home to heaven anigh
For song and mother-croon of bird
In hushed and happy twilight heard—
The treble of heaven's harmony—
These things he plants who plants a tree.

What does he plant who plants a tree?
He plants cool shade and tender rain,
And seed and bud of days to be,
And years that fade and flush again;

156

He plants the glory of the plain;
He plants the forest's heritage;
The harvest of a coming age;
They joy that unborn eyes shall see—
These things he plants who plants a tree.

What does he plant who plants a tree?
He plants, in sap and leaf and wood,
In love of home and loyalty
And far-cast thought of civic good—
His blessing on the neighborhood
Who in the hollow of His hand
Holds all the growth of all our land—
A nation's growth from sea to sea
Stirs in his heart who plants a tree.

91—Crossing the Bar

ALFRED TENNYSON
(Born August 6, 1809; Died October 6, 1892)

Sunset and evening star,
  And one clear call for me!
And may there be no moaning of the bar,
  When I put out to sea,

But such a tide as moving seems asleep,
  Too full for sound and foam,
When that which drew from out the boundless deep
  Turns again home.

Twilight and evening bell,
  And after that the dark!
And may there be no sadness of farewell,
  When I embark;

For tho' from out our bourne of Time and Place
  The flood may bear me far,

I hope to see my Pilot face to face
  When I have crost the bar.

92—Soliloquy from "Hamlet"

WILLIAM SHAKESPEARE
(Born April 26, 1564; Died April 23; 1616)

To be, or not to be—that is the question:
Whether 'tis nobler in the mind to suffer
The slings and arrows of outrageous fortune,
Or to take arms against a sea of troubles
And by opposing end them. To die, to sleep—
No more; and by a sleep to say we end
The heart-ache, and the thousand natural shocks
That flesh is heir to; 'tis a consummation
Devoutly to be wished. To die, to sleep—
To sleep—perchance to dream: ay, there's the rub;
For in that sleep of death what dreams may come,
When we have shuffled off this mortal coil,
Must give us pause: There's the respect
That makes calamity of so long life;
For who would bear the whips and scorns of time,
The oppressor's wrong, the proud man's contumely
The pangs of despised love, the law's delay,
The insolence of office, and the spurns
That patient merit of the unworthy takes,
When he himself might his quietus make
With a bare bodkin? Who would fardels bear,
To grunt and sweat under a weary life,
But that the dread of something after death,
The undiscovered country, from whose bourn
No traveler returns, puzzles the will
And makes us rather bear those ills we have
Than fly to others that we know not of?
Thus conscience does make cowards of us all,
And thus the native hue of resolution
Is sicklied o'er with the pale cast of thought,
And enterprise of great pitch and moment

With this regard their currents turn awry,
And lose the name of action

93—She Was a Phantom of Delight

WILLIAM WORDSWORTH
(Born April 7, 1770; Died April 23, 1850)

She was a phantom of delight
When first she gleamed upon my sight;
A lovely apparition, sent
To be a moment's ornament;
Her eyes as stars of twilight fair;
Like twilight's, too, her dusky hair;
But all things else about her drawn
From May-time and the cheerful dawn;
A dancing shape, an image gay,
To haunt, to startle, and way-lay.

I saw her upon a nearer view,
A spirit, yet a woman too!
Her household motions light and free,
And steps of virgin liberty;
A countenance in which did meet
Sweet records, promises as sweet;
A creature not too bright or good
For human nature's daily food;
For transient sorrows, simple wiles,
Praise, blame, love, kisses, tears and smiles.

And now I see with eye serene
The very pulse of the machine;
A being breathing thoughtful breath,
A traveler between life and death;
The reason firm, the temperate will,
Endurance, foresight, strength, and skill;
A perfect woman, nobly planned,
To warm, to comfort, and command;

159

And yet a Spirit still, and bright,
With something of angelic light.

94—The Spider and the Fly

(A Fable)

MARY HOWITT
(Born March 12, 1799; Died January 30, 1888)

"Will you walk into my parlor?" said the Spider to the Fly,
" 'Tis the prettiest little parlor that ever you did spy.
The way into my parlor is up a winding stair,
And I've a many pretty things to show when you are there."
"Oh no, no," said the little fly, "to ask me is in vain,
For who goes up your winding stair can ne'er come down again."

"I'm sure you must be weary, dear, with soaring up so high;
Will you rest upon my little bed?' said the spider to the fly.
"There are pretty curtains drawn around; the sheets are fine and thin,
And if you like to rest awhile, I'll snugly tuck you in!"
"Oh no, no," said the little fly, "for I've often heard it said,
They *never, never wake* again, who sleep upon *your* bed!"

Said the cunning spider to the fly, "Dear friend, what shall I do,
To prove the warm affection I've always felt for you?
I have within my pantry, good store of all that's nice;
I'm sure you're very welcome; will you please to take a slice?"
"Oh no, no," said the little fly, "kind sir, that cannot be;
I've heard what's in your pantry, and I do not wish to see!"
"Sweet creature!" said the spider, "you're witty and you're wise,
How handsome are your gauzy wings, how brilliant are your eyes!
I have a little looking-glass upon my parlor shelf,
If you'll step in one moment, dear, you shall behold yourself."
"I thank you, gentle sir," she said, "for what you're pleased to say,
And bidding you good morning *now*, I'll call *another* day."

The spider turned him round about, and went into his den,
For well he knew the silly fly would soon come back again:

160

So he wove a subtle web, in a little corner sly,
And set his table ready, to dine upon the fly.
Then he came out to his door again, and merrily did sing,
"Come hither, hither, pretty fly, with the pearl and silver wing;
Your robes are green and purple—there's a crest upon your head;
Your eyes are like the diamond bright, but mine are dull as lead!"

Alas, alas! how very soon this silly little fly,
Hearing his wily, flattering words, came slowly flitting by;
With buzzing wings she hung aloft, then near and nearer drew,
Thinking only of her brilliant eyes, and green and purple hue;
Thinking only of her crested head—*poor foolish thing!* At last,
Up jumped the cunning spider, and fiercely held her fast.
He dragged her up his winding stair, into his dismal den,
Within his little parlor—but she ne'er came out again!

And now dear little children, who may this story read,
To idle, silly flattering words, I pray you ne'er give heed:
Unto an evil counselor, close heart and ear and eye,
And take a lesson from this tale, of the Spider and the Fly.

95—Maud Muller

JOHN GREENLEAF WHITTIER
(Born December 17, 1807; Died September 7, 1892)

Maud Muller, on a summer's day,
Raked the meadow sweet with hay.
Beneath her torn hat glowed the wealth
Of simple beauty and rustic health.
Singing, she wrought, and her merry glee
The mock-bird echoed from his tree.

But when she glanced to the far-off town,
White from its hill-slope looking down,
The sweet song died, and a vague unrest
And a nameless longing filled her breast;
A wish, that she hardly dared to own,
For something better than she had known.

161

The Judge rode slowly down the lane,
Smoothing his horse's chestnut mane:
He drew his bridle in the shade
Of the apple-trees, to greet the maid,
And asked a draught from the spring that flowed
Through the meadow across the road.

She stooped where the cool spring bubbled up,
And filled for him her small tin cup,
And blushed as she gave it, looking down
On her feet so bare, and her tattered gown.
"Thanks!"said the Judge, "a sweeter draught
From a fairer hand was never quaffed."

He spoke of the grass, and flowers, and trees,
Of the singing birds and the humming bees;
Then talked of the haying, and wondered whether
The cloud in the west would bring foul weather.
And Maud forgot her brier-torn gown,
And her graceful ankles bare and brown,
And listened, while a pleased surprise
Looked from her long-lashed hazel eyes.

At last, like one who for delay
Seeks a vain excuse, he rode away.
Maud Muller looked and sighed: "Ah, me!
That I the Judge's bride might be!
He would dress me up in silks so fine,
And praise and toast me at his wine.

"My father should wear a broadcloth coat;
My brother should sail a painted boat;
I'd dress my mother so grand and gay,
And the baby should have a new toy each day;
And I'd feed the hungry and clothe the poor,
And all should bless me who left our door."

The Judge looked back as he climbed the hill,

And saw Maud Muller standing still.
"A form more fair, a face more sweet,
Ne'er has it been my lot to meet;
And her modest answer and graceful air
Show her wise and good as she is fair.

"Would she were mine, and I to-day,
Like her, a harvester of hay:
No doubtful balance of rights and wrongs,
Nor weary lawyers with endless tongues;
But low of cattle and song of birds,
And health, and quiet, and loving words."

But he thought of his sisters, proud and cold,
And his mother, vain of her rank and gold;
So, closing his heart, the Judge rode on,
And Maud was left in the field alone.
But the lawyers smiled that afternoon,
When he hummed in court an old-love tune;

And the young girl mused beside the well,
Till the rain on the unraked clover fell.

He wedded a wife of richest dower,
Who lived for fashion, as he for power;
Yet oft, in his marble hearth's bright glow,
He watched a picture come and go;
And sweet Maud Muller's hazel eyes.
Looked out in their innocent surprise.

Oft when the wine in his glass was red.
He longed for the wayside well instead;
And closed his eyes on his garnished rooms,
To dream of meadows and clover-blooms.
And the proud man sighed, with a secret pain,
"Ah, that I were free again!
Free as when I rode that day,
Where the barefoot maiden raked her hay."

She wedded a man unlearned and poor,
And many children played round her door;
But care and sorrow, and wasting pain,
Left their traces on heart and brain.
And oft when the summer sun shone hot
On the new-mown hay in the meadow lot,
And she heard the little spring brook fall
Over the roadside, through the wall,
In the shade of the apple-tree again
She saw a rider draw his rein,
And, gazing down with timid grace,
She felt his pleased eyes read her face.

Sometimes her narrow kitchen walls
Stretched away into stately halls;
The weary wheel to a spinet turned;
The tallow candle an astral burned;
And for him who sat by the chimney lug,
Dozing and grumbling o'er pipe and mug,
A manly form at her side she saw,
And joy was duty, and love was law.
Then she took up her burden of life again,
Saying only, "It might have been!"

Alas for maiden, alas for Judge,
For rich repiner and household drudge!
God pity them both! and pity us all,
Who vainly the dreams of youth recall;
For of all sad words of tongue or pen
The saddest are these: "It might have been!"
Ah, well! for us all some sweet hope lies
Deeply buried from human eyes;
And in the hereafter angels may
Roll the stone from its grave away!

96—The Night Before Christmas

CLEMENT MOORE
(Born July 15, 1779; Died July 10, 1863)

'Twas the night before Christmas, when all through the house
Not a creature was stirring, not even a mouse;
The stockings were hung by the chimney with care,
In hopes that St. Nicholas soon would be there;
The children were nestled all snug in their beds,
While visions of sugar-plums danced in their heads;
And Mamma in her kerchief, and I in my cap,
Had just settled our brains for a long winter's nap,
When out on the lawn there arose such a clatter,
I sprang from my bed to see what was the matter.
Away to the window I flew like a flash,
Tore open the shutters and threw up the sash.
The moon, on the breast of the new-fallen snow,
Gave a luster of mid-day to objects below;
When, what to my wandering eyes should appear,
But a miniature sleigh, and eight tiny reindeer,
With a little old driver, so lively and quick,
I knew in a moment it must be St. Nick.
More rapid than eagles his coursers they came,
And he whistled, and shouted, and called them by name:
"Now, Dasher! now, Dancer! now, Prancer and Vixen!
On, Comet! on, Cupid! on, Donder and Blitzen!
To the top of the porch, to the top of the wall!
Now, dash away, dash away, dash away, all!"
As dry leaves that before the wild hurricane fly.
When they meet with an obstacle, mount to the sky.
So, up to the house-top the coursers they flew,
With the sleigh full of toys—and St. Nicholas, too.
And then in a twinkling I heard on the roof
The prancing and pawing of each little hoof.
As I drew in my head, and was turning around,
Down the chimney St. Nicholas came with a bound.
He was dressed all in fur from his head to his foot.
And his clothes were all tarnished with ashes and soot;

165

A bundle of toys he had flung on his back,
And he looked like a peddler just opening his pack.
His eyes how they twinkled! his dimples how merry!
His cheeks were like roses, his nose like a cherry;
His droll little mouth was drawn up like a bow,
And the beard on his chin was as white as the snow.
The stump of a pipe he held tight in his teeth.
And the smoke it encircled his head like a wreath;
He had a broad face and a little round belly
That shook, when he laughed, like a bowlful of jelly.
He was chubby and plump—a right jolly old elf;
And I laughed when I saw him, in spite of myself.
A wink of his eye, and a twist of his head,
Soon gave me to know I had nothing to dread.
He spoke .not a word, but went straight to his work,
And filled all the stockings; then turned with a jerk,
And laying his finger aside of his nose,
And giving a nod, up the chimney he rose.
He sprang to his sleigh, to his team gave a whistle,
And away they all flew like the down of a thistle;
But I heard him exclaim, ere he drove out of sight,
"Happy Christmas to all, and to all a good-night!"

97—The Boys

OLIVER WENDELL HOLMES
(Born August 29, 1809; Died October 7, 1894)

Has there any old fellow got mixed with the boys?
If there has, take him out, without making a noise.
Hang the Almanac's cheat and the Catalogue's spite!
Old Time is a liar! We're twenty to-night!

We're twenty! We're twenty! Who says we are more?
He's tipsy—young jackanapes!— show him the door!
"Gray temples at twenty?"—Yes! *white* if we please;
Where the snow-flakes fall thickest there's nothing can
    freeze!

Was it snowing I spoke of? Excuse the mistake!
Look close—you will see not a sign of a flake!
We want some new garlands for those we have shed,
And these are white roses in place of the red.

We've a trick, we young fellows, you may have been told,
Of talking (in public) as if we were old;
That boy we call "Doctor," and this we call "Judge";
It's a neat little fiction—of course it's all fudge.

That fellow's the "Speaker"—the one on the right;
"Mr. Mayor," my young one, how are you to-night?
That's our "Member of Congress," we say when we chaff;
There's the "Reverend" What's-his-name?—don't make me laugh.

That boy with the grave mathematical look
Made believe he had written a wonderful book,
And the ROYAL SOCIETY thought it was *true!*
So they chose him right in; a good joke it was, too!

There's a boy, we pretend, with a three-decker brain,
That could harness a team with a logical chain;
When he spoke for our manhood in syllabled fire,
We called him "The Justice," but now he's "The Squire."

And there's a nice youngster of excellent pith:
Fate tried to conceal him by naming him Smith;
But he shouted a song for the brave and the free—
Just read on his medal, "'My country," "of thee!"

You hear that boy laughing? You think he's all fun;
But the angels laugh, too, at the good he has done.
The children laugh loud as they troop to his call,
And the poor man that knows him laughs loudest of all!

Yes, we're boys—always playing with tongue or with pen;
And I sometimes have asked, Shall we ever be men?
Shall we always be youthful and laughing and gay,
Till the last dear companion drops smiling away?

Then here's to our boyhood, its gold and its gray!
The stars of its winter, the dews of its May!
And when we have done with our life-lasting toys,
Dear Father, take care of thy children, THE BOYS!

98—My Kate

ELIZABETH BARRETT BROWNING
(Born March 6, 1806; Died June 30, 1861)

She was not as pretty as women I know,
And yet all your best made of sunshine and snow
Drop to shade, melt to nought in the long-trodden ways,
While she's still remembered on warm and cold days—

My Kate.

Her air had a meaning, her movements a grace;
You turned from the fairest to gaze on her face;
And when you had once seen her forehead and mouth,
You saw as distinctly her soul and her truth—

My Kate.

Such a blue inner light from her eyelids outbroke,
You looked at her silence and fancied she spoke;
When she did, so peculiar yet soft was the tone,
Though the loudest spoke also, you heard her alone—

My Kate.

I doubt if she said to you much that could act
As a thought or suggestion; she did not attract
In the sense of the brilliant or wise; I infer
'T was her thinking of others made you think of her—

My Kate.

She never found fault with you, never implied
Your wrong by her right; and yet men at her side
Grew nobler, girls purer, as through the whole town
The children were gladder that pulled at her gown—

My Kate.

None knelt at her feet confessed lovers in thrall;
They knelt more to God than they used—that was all;

If you praised her as charming, some asked what you meant,
But the charm of her presence was felt when she went—

> My Kate.

The weak and the gentle, the ribald and rude,
She took as she found them, and did them all good;
It always was so with her—see what you have!
She has made the grass greener even here with her grave—

> My Kate.

99—The Ballad of Jim Baxter

BY JOHN OXENHAM
(Born November 12, 1852; Died January 23, 1941)

Jim Baxter was the coarsest clay
  That ever was turned out;
But a very first-class fighting-man,
  Of that there was no doubt.

He'd fought since ever he could crawl,
  And generally won;
Because he never could be brought
  To see that he was done.

So when the war came, Jim was, off,—
  Among the first to go,
Though what the scrap was all about
  He didn't rightly know.

He simply couldn't miss it when
  There was fighting to be done.
Duty, he told the wife and kids,
  Was a thing no man could shun;
And, besides, he had a hankering
  To see the blooming fun.

And he might have been a corporal—
  Or at all events a lance,—

169

If he hadn't been, week out, week in,—
   Forever on the prance.

And he might have been a sergeant,
   If he hadn't played the goat;
For Jim was a first-class fighting-man.
   Of that there was no doubt.

And he might have been a Q.-M.-S.,
   If he hadn't been a fool;
But, though a first-class fighting-man,
   He had been no good at school.

He drank enough for ten good men,
   He swore till all was blue;
And non-coms, *never* drink or swear,
   Or do what they shouldn't do.

So Jim remained a private,—
   When he wasn't in the jug;
And hated sergeants, large and small,
   And didn't care a plug.

He liked the padre just as much,
   And heeded not his talk;
And when the good man tackled him,
   He always tried to balk.

Then came the day, when, blithe and gay,
   They smashed the German line,
And Jim was first man in the trench,
   Fighting like any nine.

They held it for an hour or more,
   While their supports in rear,
Instead of coming, lost their way,
   And threw things out of gear.

And then the huns came swarming back,

And word was given to quit;
But Jim was fighting as he drank
And paid no heed to it.

Their cartridges had given out,
Supplies had gone astray;
'T was time to go if they would live
To fight another day.

"Blank—blanketty—blank!" the Sergeant roared,—
"Back lads!—The're ten to one!"
Then something took him in the chest,—
"Back lads!" he groaned, "I'm done."

But Jim was not the kind to leave
A comrade in distress,
Although he was the awkwardest
Of all the Sergeant's mess.

So Jim, he straddled over him
And kept the huns at bay,
And, with both butt and bayonet,
Made wonderful fine play.

He fought like ten big fighting-men.
But huns have no respect
For valour in an enemy,
They deem it incorrect.

So Jim went down plugged full of holes;
But he was hard to kill,
And, while he lay unconscious, they
Worked out their evil will.

When Jim came to, he found himself
Nailed to a cross of wood,
Just like the Christ you find out there
On every country road.

He wondered dully if he'd died.
   And so become a Christ;
"Perhaps," he thought, "all men are Christs
   When they are crucified."

His strength was ebbing with his blood,
   His hands and feet were dead,
Fierce biting pains shot from the nails
   And blazed within his head.

Below, a mob of jeering huns
   Mocked at his woful plight,
They bade him loose himself, and come
   Down for another fight.

"Christ!"—groaned Jim Baxter, through his teeth,
   And meant no ill thereby;—
It was his usual expletive
   And came most readily.

"Christ!"—groaned Jim Baxter, through his teeth,
   "D'you call. . . .this. . . .fighting fair?
Just loose me hands .... and loose me feet ....
   An' I'd lick you still. . . .I swear.

"Christ!"—groaned Jim Baxter, through his teeth,
   As the pangs took hold of him,—
"I'm going quick. . . . a dirty trick...."
   His eyes were growing dim.

But, suddenly, he raised his head,
   His eyes shone clear and bright,
And opened wide. . . . for, at his side,
   Stood One clothed all in white.

The sun broke through the morning mist
   And bathed them in its light,—
Jim Baxter nailed upon his cross,
   And The Other all in white.

His face was wondrous pitiful,
  But still more wondrous sweet;
And Jim saw holes just like his own
  In His white hands and feet;
But His look it was that won Jim's heart,
  It was so wondrous sweet.

"Christ!"—said the dying man once more,
  With accent reverent,
He had never said it so before,
  But he knew now what Christ meant;—

"Christ" meant a friend in time of need,
In spite of foes,—a friend indeed;
  That was quite evident,—
A friend who drew his heart right out,
And for his soul did plead.
Jim gave in full, heart, mind and soul,
  In deep acknowledgment.

And then, through all his deadly pains,
  He bravely smiled .... and sighed,—
Just one long sigh of deep content,
  Then dropped his head .... and died.

His comrades took the trench next day,
  And found him nailed up there,
With a smile of grace upon his face,
  But never a sign of care.

And there, on his cross, they buried him,
  Against a Judgment Day;
Not That Great Day,—but a nearer one,
That draweth on as the war is won,
When, for the evil they have done,
  The doers of ill shall pay.

100—The Fool's Prayer

EDWARD R. SILL
(Born April 29, 1841; Died February 27, 1887)

The royal feast was done; the King
  Sought some new sport to banish care,
And to his jester cried: "Sir Fool,
  Kneel now, and make for us a prayer!"

The jester doffed his cap and bells,
  And stood the mocking court before;
They could not see the bitter smile
  Behind the painted grin he wore.

He bowed his head, and bent his knee
  Upon the monarch's silken stool;
His pleading voice arose: "O Lord,
  Be merciful to me, a fool!

"No pity, Lord, could change the heart
  From red with wrong to white as wool;
The rod must heal the sin: but, Lord,
  Be merciful to me, a fool!

" 'Tis not by guilt the onward sweep
  Of truth and right, O Lord, we stay;
'Tis by our follies that so long
  We hold the earth from heaven away.

"These clumsy feet, still in the mire,
  Go crushing blossoms without end;
These hard, well-meaning hands we thrust
  Among the heart-strings of a friend.

"The ill-timed truth we might have kept—
  Who knows how sharp it pierced and stung?
The word we had not sense to say—
  Who knows how grandly it had rung?

174

"Our faults no tenderness should ask,
    The chastening stripes must cleanse them all;
But for our blunders—oh, in shame
    Before the eyes of heaven we fall.

"Earth bears no balsam for mistakes;
    Men crown the knave, and scourge the tool
That did his will; but Thou, O Lord,
    Be merciful to me, a fool!"

The room was hushed; in silence rose
    The King, and sought his gardens cool,
And walked apart, and murmured low,
    "Be merciful to me, a fool!"

101—To a Waterfowl

WILLIAM CULLEN BRYANT
(Born November 3, 1794; Died June 12, 1878)

Whither, 'midst falling dew,
    While glow the heavens with the last steps of day,
Far, through their rosy depths, dost thou pursue
    Thy solitary way?

Vainly the fowler's eye
    Might mark thy distant flight to do thee wrong,
As, darkly painted on the crimson sky,
    Thy figure floats along.

Seek'st thou the plashy brink
    Of weedy lake, or marge of river wide,
Or where the rocking billows rise and sink
    On the chafed ocean's side?

There is a Power whose care
    Teaches thy way along that pathless coast—

The desert and illimitable air—
   Lone wandering, but not lost.

All day thy wings have fanned,
   At that far height, the cold, thin atmosphere,
Yet stoop not weary, to the welcome land,
   Though the dark night is near.

And soon that toil shall end;
   Soon shalt thou find a summer home, and rest,
And scream among thy fellows; reeds shall bend,
   Soon, o'er thy sheltered nest.

Thou'rt gone! the abyss of heaven
   Hath swallowed up thy form; yet on my heart
Deeply hath sunk the lesson thou hast given,
   And shall not soon depart.

He who, from zone to zone,
   Guides through the boundless sky thy certain flight,
In the long way that I must tread alone
   Will lead my steps aright.

102—I Shall not Pass this Way Again

(A Symphony)

EVA ROSE YORK
(Born December 22, 1858, Died 1935)

I shall not pass this way again—
   Although it bordered be with flowers,
Although I rest in fragrant bowers,
    And hear the singing
    Of song-birds winging
To highest heaven their gladsome flight;
Though moons are full and stars are bright,
And winds and waves are softly sighing,
While leafy trees make low replying;

176

Though voices clear in joyous strain
Repeat a jubilant refrain;
Though rising suns their radiance throw
On summer's green and winter's snow,
In such rare splendor that my heart
Would ache from scenes like these to part;
 Though beauties heighten,
 And life-lights brighten,
And joys proceed from every pain,—
I shall not pass this way again.

Then let me pluck the flowers that blow,
And let me listen as I go
 To music rare
 That fills the air;
 And let hereafter
 Songs and laughter
Fill every pause along the way;
And to my spirit let me say:

"O soul, be happy; soon 'tis trod,
The path made thus for thee by God.
Be happy, thou, and bless His name
By whom such marvellous beauty came,"
And let no chance by me be lost
To kindness show at any cost.
I shall not pass this way again;
Then let me now relieve some pain,
Remove some barrier from the road,
Or brighten some one's heavy load;
A helping hand to this one lend,
Then turn some other to befriend.

 O God, forgive
 That now I live
As if I might, sometime, return
To bless the weary ones that yearn
For help and comfort every day,—
For there be such along the way.

177

God, forgive that I have seen
The beauty only, have not been
Awake to sorrow such as this;
That I have drunk the cup of bliss
Remembering not that those there be
Who drink the dregs of misery.

I love the beauty of the scene,
Would roam again o'er fields so green;
But since I may not, let me spend
My strength for others to the end,—
For those who tread on rock and stone,
And bear their burdens all alone,
Who loiter not in leafy bowers,
Nor hear the birds nor pluck the flowers.
A larger kindness give to me,
A deeper love and sympathy;
    Then, Oh, one day
    May someone say—
Remembering a lessened pain—
Would she could pass this way again."

103—Apostrophe to the Ocean

From "Childe Harold's Pilgrimage"

GEORGE GORDON BYRON
(Born January 22, 1788; Died April 19, 1824)

There is a pleasure in the pathless woods,
  There is a rapture on the lonely shore,
There is society where none intrudes,
  By the deep sea, and music in its roar.
  I love not man the less, but Nature more,
From these our interviews, in which I steal
  From all I may be, or have been before,
To mingle with the universe, and feel
What I can ne'er express, yet can not all conceal.

Roll on, thou deep and dark blue ocean, roll!
  Ten thousand fleets sweep over thee in vain;
Man marks the earth with ruin, his control
  Stops with the shore; upon the watery plain
  The wrecks are all thy deed, nor doth remain
A shadow of man's ravage, save his own,
  When for a moment, like a drop of rain,
He sinks into thy depths with bubbling groan,
Without a grave, unknelled, uncoffined, and unknown.

His steps are not upon thy paths, thy fields
  Are not a spoil for him,—thou dost arise
And shake him from thee; the vile strength he wields
  For earth's destruction thou dost all despise,
  Spurning him from thy bosom to the skies,
And send'st him, shivering in thy playful spray
  And howling, to his Gods, where haply lies
His petty hope in some near port or bay,
And dashst him again to earth:—there let him lay.

The armaments which thunder-strike the walls
  Of rock-built cities, bidding nations quake,
And monarchs tremble in their capitals;
  The oak leviathans, whose huge ribs make
  Their clay creator the vain title take
Of lord of thee, and arbiter of war;—
  These are thy toys, and, as the snowy flake,
They melt into, the yest of waves, which mar
Alike the Armada's pride or spoils of Trafalgar.

Thy shores are empires, changed in all save thee;
  Assyria, Greece, Rome, Carthage—what are they?
Thy waters wasted them while they were free,
  And many a tyrant since; their shores obey
  The stranger, slave, or savage; their decay
Has dried up realms to deserts: not so thou,
  Unchangeable save to thy wild waves' play;

Time writes no wrinkle on thy azure brow;
Such as creation's dawn beheld, thou rollest now.

Thou glorious mirror, where the Almighty's form
   Glasses itself in tempests; in all time.
Calm or convulsed; in breeze, or gale, or storm,
   Icing the pole, or in the torrid clime,
   Dark-heaving; boundless, endless, and sublime;—
The image of Eternity, the throne
   Of the Invisible; even from out thy slime
The monsters of the deep are made; each zone
Obeys thee; thou goest forth, dread, fathomless, alone.

And I have loved thee. Ocean! and my joy
   Of youthful sports, was on thy breast to be
Borne, like thy bubbles, onward: from a boy
   I wanton'd with thy breakers—they to me
   Were a delight; and if the freshening sea
Made them a terror—'twas a pleasing fear,
   For I was as it were a child of thee,
And trusted to thy billows far and near,
And laid my hand upon thy mane—as I do here.

Made in the USA
Columbia, SC
18 January 2019